Lively

SUCCESSFUL CHRISTIAN PARENTING

Raising Your Child with Care,
Compassion, and Common Sense

SUCCESSFUL CHRISTIAN PARENTING

Raising Your Child with Care,
Compassion, and Common Sense

BY JOHN MACARTHUR

WORD PUBLISHING

NASHVILLE

A Thomas Nelson Company

To my beloved grandchildren,
whose parents are already bringing them up
in the nurture and admonition of the Lord.
May none of them ever depart from the way.

—PROVERBS 22:6

CONTENTS

INTRODUCTION

NEARLY TWO DECADES AGO I preached a series of sermons entitled "The Fulfilled Family." That brief study from Ephesians 5 has proved to be by far the most popular sermon series I have ever preached. It was the basis for one of my early books, *The Family*,[1] and an accompanying video series. We've broadcast those original sermons several times over the years on the "Grace to You" radio broadcast, and they never fail to elicit an overwhelming response.

A large part of that response consists of letters from parents seeking more specific help on issues related to parenting. Here is where biblical living becomes most practical and most urgent. Christian parents do not want to fail at raising their children in the nurture and admonition of the Lord, but the potential pitfalls can seem overwhelming. One young father recently wrote this to me:

> I'm looking for *biblical* help with parenting. Not just parenting advice from a Christian perspective, not just warmed-over child psychology couched in "Christian" terminology, but solid, biblical parenting guidelines.
>
> It seems to me that the specific *commandments* to fathers in the Bible can be written on half a sheet of paper. But I'm sure there are also *principles* in Scripture that teach parents how to raise their kids. I'm just

having a hard time knowing which "principles" are really biblical and which are not. I looked for parenting books in the Christian bookstore. There were lots of choices, but I notice they are peppered with phrases like "your child's sense of self-worth"; "self-bias impulse drive"; "attention deficit disorder"; and so on. How much of this is truly biblical, and how much is borrowed from secular child psychology? I see very little in these books that actually refers to the Scriptures.

My wife and I are barely out of our teenage years, and now we are faced with the responsibility for training up our child in the way that he should go. I don't feel we are quite ready for the task. Can you recommend some resources that will help us?

I remember vividly when our eldest son was born what it was like to suddenly *feel* the enormous weight of responsibility that comes with parenthood. My own children are now grown and have themselves embarked on the adventure of parenting. It is a delight to see them beginning to raise their little ones in the nurture and admonition of the Lord. Watching my own grandchildren begin to grow often reminds me just what an imposing task parenting is, not only for young parents just starting out, but often even more so for parents of adolescents and young adults.

I can sympathize, too, with that young father's bewilderment in looking over the various options that are being set forth as "Christian parenting" today. The market is flooded with questionable or outright wrongheaded approaches to child-rearing. We are faced with a glut of so-called "Christian" parenting helps, but truly *biblical* resources are rare indeed.

Meanwhile, Christian families are self-destructing all around. As society has waded deeper into the morass of humanism and secularism, the church has too often failed to stand against the perilous tide.

Unfortunately, the impact of widespread worldliness and compromise in the church is taking a toll on Christian families.

This is a serious crisis. The family is the germ-cell of civilization, and we may be witnessing its death throes. The media parades evidence of this before us all the time: divorce, the sexual revolution, abortion, sterilization, delinquency, infidelity, homosexuality, women's liberation, children's rights, the glorification of rebellion.

Meanwhile, secular society, and at times even our federal government, seems intent on redefining and reshaping the very idea of family. Same-sex marriages, homosexual couples adopting kids, the global village concept, and other radical approaches to family life actually undermine the family while using the language of family values. Politicians seem more and more intent on usurping the parental role. And parents seem more and more willing to abdicate that role to others.

More than ever, Christians need to know what the Bible teaches about parenting and begin to put it to practice.

This is not a book on child psychology. It is unlike the pragmatic or formulaic approaches to parenting and family life. I am proposing no new *method*. Instead, my goal is to present the principles of *biblical* parenting with as much clarity as possible, and help to make sense of parents' duties before God. I'm convinced that if Christian parents understand and apply the simple principles Scripture sets forth, they can rise above the trends of secular society and bring up their children in a way that honors Christ, in any culture and under any circumstances.

ONE

Shade for Our Children

Bring them up in the nurture and admonition of the Lord.

—EPHESIANS 6:4, KJV

ONE

Shade for Our Children

An old Chinese proverb says, "One generation plants the trees and another gets the shade." Our generation lives in the shade of many trees that were planted by our ancestors.

In spiritual terms, we derive shade from our parents' and grandparents' ethical standards, their perceptions of right and wrong, their sense of moral duty, and above all, their spiritual commitment. Their ideals determined the kind of civilization we inherited from them, and our generation's ideals will likewise shape tomorrow's culture for our kids.

There's no question that society as a whole is in a serious state of moral and spiritual decline. So the question that faces Christian parents today is whether we can plant some trees that will shade future generations from what may well be the blistering heat of anti-Christian values in an anti-Christian world. Are we planting the right kind of shade trees, or are we leaving our children totally exposed?

THE DEMISE OF MODERN SOCIETY

It should be obvious to anyone who has any commitment to the truth of Scripture that our culture as a whole is rapidly disintegrating morally, ethically, and above all spiritually. The values now embraced by society as a whole are badly out of sync with God's divine order.

For example, the American court system sanctions the wholesale massacring of millions of unborn children annually, but a court in Kansas City recently sentenced one woman to four months in jail for killing a litter of unwanted kittens.[1] A court in Janesville, Wisconsin, sentenced a man to twelve years in prison for killing five cats "to relieve stress."[2] The case was indeed a heinous example of cruelty to animals. But two days after that man began serving his twelve-year prison sentence, a Delaware court sentenced a woman to only thirty months in prison for killing her newborn infant. The woman had tossed the newborn child out a third-floor motel-room window into a garbage bin in the alley below, umbilical cord still attached. Evidence showed the baby was alive when thrown out the window but died of exposure, abandonment, and massive skull fractures.[3]

It is clear that our society as a whole no longer believes humans are made in the image of God, very different from animals.

In fact, the increasing popularity of the animal-rights lobby perfectly illustrates how far our society has moved from its moorings of biblical principles. Even while this movement continues to gain unprecedented popularity, it grows more and more radical, and more and more outspoken against the biblical view of humanity. Ingrid Newkirk, founder of People for the Ethical Treatment of Animals (PETA), says, "There is no rational basis for saying that a human being has special rights. When it comes to having a central nervous system, and the ability to feel pain, hunger, and thirst, a rat is a pig is a dog is a boy."[4] Newkirk sees no difference between the atrocities of World War II and killing animals for food: "Six million Jews died in concentration camps, but six *billion* broiler chickens will die this year in slaughterhouses."[5]

Such ideas are gaining widespread approval in mainstream society. Some of our culture's best-known and most respected celebrities parrot similar thoughts, usually under the guise of compassion. But such a skewed perspective of "kindness" to animals quickly becomes wanton unkindness to creatures made in God's image. The inevitable impact such thinking will have on the legacy today's parents leave the next generation is hinted at in a remark made by Michael Fox, vice president of the Humane Society of the United States. He says, "The life of an ant and the life of my child should be granted equal consideration."[6] What kind of values will our children's culture have?

Society is full of similar frightening trends. The future is unthinkable for a society without any moral standard by which to determine right and wrong. Already we are willing to sentence people to prison for killing animals, while encouraging abortionists to kill children.

Where is our culture going? What kind of value system, what kind of morality, what kind of world are we establishing for the next generation?

And as Christians, are we planting any shade trees for our children? Or are we leaving them totally exposed?

THE DEMISE OF THE FAMILY

We may be watching the death of the germ-cell of all civilization, the family. Signs of the family's demise are abundantly clear all around us. Numerous facts confirm the grim prognosis. There's almost no need to cite statistics. For the past forty years or more the signs of the family's collapse have been paraded before us continually: divorce, the sexual revolution, abortion, sterilization, delinquency, infidelity, homosexuality, radical feminism, the "children's-rights" movement, together with the normalization of the single-parent home, the decline of the nuclear family, and other similar signs. We have been watching the braiding of an intricate rope that will ultimately strangle the family to death.

To be perfectly frank, many people today would happily carve out the tombstone for the family. In his 1971 book, *The Death of the Family*,[7] British psychiatrist Dr. David Cooper suggested that it is time to do away with the family completely. A similar suggestion was made in Kate Millet's 1970 feminist manifesto, *Sexual Politics*.[8] She claimed that families, along with all patriarchal structures, must go because they are nothing more than tools for the oppression and enslavement of women.

Most of the people touting such perspectives are aggressive, angry, and determined to impose their agendas on the rest of society. The most fertile ground for the propagation of such viewpoints is the university campus. Consequently, the proponents of anti-family social engineering are busily reeducating the young people who will soon be the main leaders of society and the parents of a generation that will probably be even more dysfunctional than the current one.

This sort of indoctrination has been going on for many years, so that some of the most influential people already shaping modern society at the highest levels—from government leaders to those who make network television's programming decisions—are some of the most virulent and outspoken enemies of the traditional family.

Hillary Rodham Clinton, for example, would like to hand over to the federal government some of the rights and responsibilities of child rearing. Mrs. Clinton's book, *It Takes a Village*,[9] was written to set forth an agenda that would move America closer to state-sponsored parenting. Although she gives lip service to the importance of the parents' and grandparents' roles, she clearly believes that parents should not be permitted to train their own children unsupervised by the secular government. She also suggests that a more socialist approach to parenting should be the new norm, including state-sponsored day-care centers and full-day preschools for children as young as three. It appears that the village Mrs. Clinton envisions is a morass of federally-funded programs designed to indoctrinate children with whatever values the state deems acceptable. And if anything has been made clear over the past half century, it is that biblical values are certainly *not* deemed acceptable in any government-sponsored program in America, so Mrs. Clinton's village would no doubt indoctrinate children with secular humanism instead.

Other voices are calling for even more radical measures against the traditional family. Ti-Grace Atkinson, former president of the New York chapter of the National Organization for Women, says she would like to eliminate all sex, marriage, motherhood, and love. "Marriage is legalized servitude," she says, "and family relations are the basis for all human oppression."[10]

Gore Vidal, best-selling author and social critic, agrees. He proposes reorganizing society to eliminate the family as we now know it. Instead, he would like to see a central *authority* with the power to control human population, food distribution, and the use of natural resources.[11]

IS IT TOO LATE TO SAVE THE FAMILY?

Fortunately, the voices calling for such Orwellian alternatives to the family are still in the minority. Even secular sociologists for the most part regard the decline of the family as an unmitigated disaster. Most agree that the family is a crucial building block for civilized society, and they freely admit that if the family does not survive—and thrive—as an institution, the demise of society itself cannot be far behind.

Consequently in virtually every public forum these days, we're beginning to hear knowledgeable people talk about the need to shore up the family. Sociologists, psychologists, analysts, so-called marriage and family experts, and all the rest are scrambling to come up with solutions for what ails the family. I'm speaking now about secular, non-Christian voices, yet they are expressing concern about the number of families that are breaking up and the inevitable negative effect this has on society. They note with concern the increasing numbers of latch-key children—kids who come home daily to unsupervised, parentless homes. They express fears about the dramatic rise in serious crimes committed by young children. They are cautioning us that parental permissiveness, relaxed moral standards, and other liberalizing social influences have already resulted in the demise of many families and some whole communities. And if not corrected, these problems will destroy society as we know it.

Anyone can see that most of these problems are directly related to the breakdown of values once nurtured in the family. It has become painfully obvious that such ills are not merely social problems requiring public-sector solutions, but they are, first of all, *family* problems, whose solutions depend on the rescue of the family as an institution.

The problem is that society as a whole has already rejected the biblical values that are necessary for the recovery and preservation of the family. The term "family values" is a scorned and much-abused phrase, derided by some as a propaganda tool, hijacked by others who advocate values that are absolutely detrimental to the family.

But the truth is, the only real *values* that can save the family are rooted in Scripture—they are *biblical* values, not just *family* values.

Therefore the future of the family in our society hinges on the success of those who are committed to the truth of Scripture. Various secular experts have been proposing their humanistic "solutions" to society's problems for years, with virtually no impact. The secular experts will never uncover any solution outside Scripture that will heal those woes. No such solution exists.

Meanwhile, as human relationships continue to deteriorate within families, the very fabric of society is being torn apart. (Watch any random episode of "The Jerry Springer Show," and you're likely to see troubling evidence that this is the case.) Conversely, if society itself is to grow stronger, the turnaround must begin in our families.

Unfortunately, society itself may pose the biggest obstacle to the reform of the family. Consider the following anti-family values our society has already canonized. All of these are fairly new developments within the past half-century:

- All taboos are systematically being abolished and replaced with one new taboo: Absolute moral standards, instituted by God and revealed in the Bible, should govern all human behavior.

- Divorce is available on demand for any reason, or for no reason at all.

- Since gender differences are supposed to be downplayed and eliminated as much as possible, it's now improper to speak of "headship" in the family as a masculine responsibility.

- Married women with children are encouraged to work outside the home.

- Entertainment, and television in particular, dominates home life.

- Killing a baby seal for fur is criminal; yet killing unborn human infants for any reason whatsoever is defended as a matter of free, personal choice.

- Pornography of the most debauched sort is protected in America under the First Amendment while teaching children in public schools that sexual promiscuity is immoral is prohibited as a violation of the Constitution.

Can a society committed to such values save its own failing families? Not much common sense is needed to see that the seeds of the family's destruction are built right into the moral values our culture has embraced over the past generation. It would seem obvious that unless society itself is utterly transformed through the kind of sweeping revival early America experienced during the First Great Awakening, the future of the family as an institution in this culture is in serious trouble.

WHERE IS THE CHURCH IN ALL OF THIS?

I'm certainly not suggesting that the family might be saved by moral reform in a secular culture. This is not a rallying cry for Christians to be more aggressive in pursuing political action. Far too much of the church's efforts in recent years has been squandered trying to confront anti-family trends, such as abortion and homosexuality, through legislative efforts alone. *Reform* is no answer for a culture like ours. *Redemption* is what is needed, and that occurs at the individual, not societal, level. The church needs to get back to the real task to which we are called: evangelizing the lost. Only when multitudes of individuals in our society turn to Christ will society itself experience any significant transformation.

Meanwhile, Christian families have an obligation to plant shade trees for future generations of children. But, frankly, even in the church, the family's condition looks pretty bleak.

Not that there aren't positive signs. For nearly three decades there has been a tremendous preoccupation among evangelicals with the need to rescue the family. Christian bookstores are well-stocked with books on marriage and the family. Christian radio is also crowded with family-oriented programming. For more than two decades running, the most popular Christian broadcast (by far) has been "Focus on the Family." There is no shortage of Christian programs, seminars, and ministries devoted to the family and parenting.

Despite all the ink and air time such ministries have devoted to the subjects of parenting and the family, though, statistics still show that in general, Christian families are not in much better shape than the families of their non-Christian neighbors. According to some pollsters, the divorce rate among evangelicals may actually be a few percentage points *higher* than in the world at large. The percentage of single-parent families is already higher in the church than in the world. Children from Christian families are not immune to the lure of drugs, gangs, promiscuous sex, and all the other evils plaguing the youth of today. By and large, Christian families are suffering from all the same woes as non-Christian families.

Something is clearly wrong.

Part of the problem is that many of the parenting and family programs being labeled "Christian" today are not truly Christian. Some are nothing more than secular behaviorism papered over with a religious veneer—an unholy amalgam of biblical-sounding expressions blended with humanistic psychology. Even some of the better Christian parenting programs focus far too much on relatively petty extrabiblical matters and not enough on the essential biblical principles. One book I consulted spent chapter after chapter on issues like how to make a chore list to hang on the refrigerator, how to organize your child's schedule to limit television time, games to play in the car, and similar how-to advice. Such pragmatic concerns may have their place, but they don't go to the heart of what Christian parents in a society like ours need to address. (That particular book actually had very little that was distinctively Christian, outside the author's preface.)

Some Christian parenting programs seem to begin well but quickly move away from biblical principles and into other things. Those *other things* often receive more stress than more vital issues that *are* truly biblical. Parents who sign up for such programs demand detailed, heavily regimented programs or turnkey parenting systems that work right out of the box. So that is what the experts try to produce. The resulting lists of rules and how-tos quickly supersede the vital biblical principles. The lure in this direction is subtle but strong, and rare is the parenting guru who successfully avoids it.

What we desperately need is a return to the *biblical* principles of parenting. Christian parents don't need new, shrink-wrapped programs; they need to apply and obey consistently the few simple principles that are clearly set forth for parents in God's Word, such as these: Constantly teach your kids the truth of God's Word (Deuteronomy 6:7). Discipline them when they do wrong (Proverbs 23:13–14). And don't provoke them to anger (Colossians 3:21). Those few select principles alone, if consistently applied, would have a far greater positive impact for the typical struggling parent than hours of discussion about whether babies should be given pacifiers, or what age kids should be before they're permitted to choose their own clothes, or dozens of similar issues that consume so much time in the typical parenting program.

Throughout this book we'll be closely examining those biblical parenting principles and others. We begin with four oft-neglected biblical principles that should lay the foundation for the Christian parent's perspective.

CHILDREN SHOULD BE SEEN AS A BLESSING, NOT A HARDSHIP

First, Scripture clearly teaches that children are blessed gifts from the Lord. God designed them to be a blessing. They are supposed to be a joy. They are a benediction from the Lord to grace our lives with fulfillment, meaning, happiness, and satisfaction. Parenthood is God's gift to us.

This is true even in a fallen world, infected with the curse of sin. In the midst of all that's evil, children are tokens of God's lovingkindness. They are living proof that God's mercy extends even to fallen, sinful creatures.

Remember that Adam and Eve ate the forbidden fruit *before* they had conceived any offspring. Yet God did not simply destroy them and start over with a new race. Instead, he permitted Adam and Eve to fulfill the command given them before the Fall: Be fruitful and multiply (Genesis 1:28). And He set in motion a plan of redemption that would ultimately embrace untold numbers of Adam's offspring (Revelation 7:9–10). The children Eve bore therefore embodied the hope that fallen sinners could be redeemed.

And when God cursed the earth because of Adam's sin, He multiplied the *pain* of the childbirth process (Genesis 3:16), but he did not nullify the *blessing* inherent in bearing children.

Eve recognized this. Genesis 4:1 says, "Now Adam knew Eve his wife, and she conceived and bore Cain, and said, 'I have acquired a man from the LORD.'" She clearly recognized that the Lord was the source of this child. She regarded the child as a gift from the hand of the One whom she had sinned against, and she was overjoyed by it. Despite the pain of childbirth, and irrespective of the fallenness of the child himself, she knew that the child was an emblem of God's grace to her.

In verse 25 we read, "And Adam knew his wife again, and she bore a son and named him Seth, 'For God has appointed another seed for me.'" Children, Eve knew, are blessed gifts from God.

What of the children of unbelievers? They represent divine blessings, too. In Genesis 17:20 God promised to bless Ishmael. How would He bless him? By multiplying his children and descendants. He told Abraham, "And as for Ishmael, I have heard you. Behold, I have blessed him, and will make him fruitful, and will multiply him exceedingly."

Throughout Scripture we find a running theme that highlights children as blessings from the hand of a loving and merciful God. This becomes evident, for example, in the contest between Leah and Rachel for Jacob's affection. Genesis 29:31–33 says, "When the LORD saw that Leah was unloved, He opened her womb; but Rachel was barren. So Leah conceived and bore a son, and she called his name Reuben; for she said, "The LORD has surely looked on my affliction. Now therefore, my husband will love me." Then she conceived again and bore a son, and said, "Because the LORD has heard that I am unloved, He has therefore given me this son also."

Notice that the Lord's compassion for Leah is manifested by His enabling her to bear children. The Lord is the one who opened her womb, and Leah recognized this.

Meanwhile, although Jacob loved Rachel more, Rachel felt her own barrenness somehow implied that she was less favored. Scripture says, "Rachel envied her sister, and said to Jacob, 'Give me children, or else I die'" (Genesis 30:1)!

Scripture says, "And Jacob's anger was aroused against Rachel, and he said, 'Am I in the place of God, who has withheld from you the fruit of the womb'" (v. 2)? He too recognized that only God can give children.

Rachel was so determined to have children that she concocted a wrong-headed scheme by which to have *surrogate* children through her handmaid, Bilhah (v. 3), thus compounding the already sinful complexities of the polygamous relationship that was the source of her strife with Leah in the first place. In the end, God blessed Rachel with children, too, and she praised Him for His goodness to her: "And she conceived and bore a son, and said, 'God has taken away my reproach'" (v. 23). Rachel died giving birth to Benjamin, and her midwife offered these words of dying comfort: "Do not fear; you will have this son also" (35:17).

Throughout this tale of the parents who gave birth to the various tribes of God's chosen people, one thing is clear: All parties understood that children signified the blessings of the Lord.

By God's gracious design, children are given to bring parents joy, happiness, contentment, satisfaction, and love. Psalm 127:3–5 says so expressly:

> Behold, children are a gift of the Lord,
> The fruit of the womb is a reward.
> Like arrows in the hand of a warrior,
> So are the children of one's youth.
> How blessed is the man whose quiver is full of them;
> They will not be ashamed
> When they speak with their enemies in the gate.

Clearly, in the plan of God, children are meant to be a blessing, not a hardship. And they usually are a blessing when they arrive. But left exposed to this world and unshaded by the proper kind of protection, they will indeed break your heart.

That leads to the second foundational principle.

PARENTING IS SUPPOSED TO BE A JOY, NOT A BURDEN

The parent's task is not a yoke to be borne; it is a privilege to be enjoyed. If God's design in giving us children is to bless us, the task He calls us to as parents is nothing more than an extension and magnification of that blessing.

Parenting is hard only to the degree that parents *make* it hard by failing to follow the simple principles God sets forth. To neglect one's duty before God as a parent is to forfeit the blessing inherent in the task, and those who do so take on a burden God never intended parents to bear.

One sure way to fill your life with misery is to abdicate the responsibility God has given you as a parent and a steward of the child He has graciously placed into your hands. Conversely, nothing in your life will engender more sheer joy and gladness than bringing up your children in the nurture and admonition of the Lord.

Are there no inherently distasteful aspects to parenting? Of course, none of us takes delight in having to discipline our children. I quickly learned as a parent that what my parents always told me about discipline was right: It usually pains the parent more than it pains the child. But even the discipline process ultimately produces joy when we are faithful to God's instructions. Proverbs 29:17 says, "Correct your son, and he will give you rest; yes, he will give delight to your soul."

There's a refreshing, exhilarating wealth of rich joy in godly parenting that cannot be acquired by any other means. God has graciously designed into the parenting process a fountain of delight, if we abide by His principles.

Does Scripture guarantee that our parenting will succeed if we follow God's plan? Consider this third foundational point.

SUCCESS IN PARENTING IS MEASURED BY WHAT THE PARENTS DO, NOT BY WHAT THE CHILD DOES

If we measure our success as parents solely by what our children become, there is no inviolable guarantee in Scripture that we will experience absolute success on those terms. Sometimes children raised in fine Christian families grow up to abandon the faith. On the other hand, the Lord graciously redeems many children whose parents are utter failures. The outcome of the child, as a factor taken by itself, is no reliable gauge of the parents' success.

However, the *true* measure of success for Christian parents is the parents' own character. To the degree that we have followed God's design for parenting, we have succeeded as parents before God.

Invariably parents ask about Proverbs 22:6: "Train up a child in the way he should go, and when he is old he will not depart from it." Isn't that a biblical promise that if we raise our children right, we can guarantee that they will walk faithfully with the Lord?

That notion is based on a misunderstanding of the nature of the Proverbs. These are wise sayings and truisms—not necessarily inviolable rules. For example, two verses earlier, we read, "By humility and the fear of the LORD are riches and honor and life" (v. 4). That is certainly not a blanket promise that everyone who is humble and fears the Lord will always be rich and receive honor. Too many other verses also teach us that the righteous are inevitably persecuted (2 Timothy 3:12) and often poor (James 2:5).

Furthermore, Proverbs 10:27 says, "The fear of the LORD prolongs days, but the years of the wicked will be shortened." We know that this principle does not hold true in every case. It cannot be claimed as if it were a binding promise from God to all who fear the Lord.

Likewise, Proverbs 22:6 is a principle that is generally true. The same principle would be true if applied to soldiers, carpenters, teachers, or any other form of training. How a person is trained determines what he becomes. In Jesus' words, "Everyone, after he has been fully trained, will be like his teacher" (Luke 6:40, NASB). The same principle applies to children, who are also, normally, products of their training. This is an axiomatic or self-evident truism.

But Proverbs 22:6 is not a promise for Christian parents to claim that will guarantee their children will never depart from the way of truth. The great Puritan commentator Matthew Henry made these remarks about the truism of Proverbs 22:6, "When they *grow up,* when they *grow old,* it is to be hoped, they *will not depart from it.* Good impressions made upon them then will abide upon them all their days. Ordinarily the vessel retains the savour with which it was first seasoned. Many indeed have departed from the good way in which they were trained up; Solomon himself did so. But early training may be a means of their recovering themselves, as it is supposed Solomon did. At least the parents will have the comfort of having done their duty and used the means."[12]

As a general rule, parents who follow biblical principles in bringing up their children *will* see a positive effect on the character of their children. From a purely statistical point of view, children who grow up in Christ-honoring homes are more likely to remain faithful to Christ in adulthood than kids growing up in homes where the parents dishonor the Lord. The truism of Proverbs 22:6 does apply. We're certainly not to think that God's sovereignty in salvation means the way we raise our kids is immaterial. God often uses faithful parents as instruments in the salvation of children.

Ultimately, however, your children's salvation *is* a matter to be settled between them and God. Nothing you can do will *guarantee* your kids' salvation. To that end you should be praying to God and instructing your child—using all available means to impress the truths of the gospel perpetually on the child's heart. But ultimately a grown child's spiritual fitness alone is not necessarily a reliable gauge of the parents' success.

Having said that, I want to stress that sometimes—I should say *often*—parents *are* partly to blame for their wayward children's rebellion. And it has been my observation over the years that parents are generally more to blame for wayward kids than society, or peers, or any of the other influences parents tend to blame. I occasionally encounter parents who have violated nearly every biblical principle of parenting, who nonetheless come to the pastor seeking some kind of absolution from the responsibility for their children's defiance. They want verbal assurance that they are in no way to blame; someone else is.

Yet God Himself has given the responsibility for raising children to parents—not to schoolteachers, peers, child-care workers, or other people outside the family—and therefore it is wrong for parents to attempt to unload that responsibility or shift the blame when things go wrong. This is the fourth foundational principle.

A CHILD'S MOST IMPORTANT INFLUENCES COME FROM PARENTS, NOT PEERS

God has solemnly charged parents with the duty of raising their children in the nurture and admonition of the Lord. It is not the parent's prerogative to delegate that duty to others. Parents must involve themselves in their children's lives enough to insure that *no other influence* takes precedence. To parents who complain that their kids' failures are the kids' friends' fault, my inevitable reply is that ultimately the parents themselves must therefore be to blame, because they were the ones who allowed peers to have more input into their kids' lives than they have themselves.

Some parents will no doubt cynically roll their eyes at that, and insist that it is unrealistic in this day and age to expect parents to influence their kids more than peers, the culture, television, school-teachers, and all the other factors that vie for a controlling interest in the typical child's life.

A similar cynicism is expressed in a recently-published book, *The Nurture Assumption: Why Children Turn Out the Way They Do,*[13] by Judith Rich Harris, a New Jersey-based grandmother and author of several psychology textbooks. She insists that virtually nothing parents can do will make any significant difference in their child's temperament, personality, or character. "Parenting has been oversold," she says. "You have been led to believe that you have more of an influence on your child's personality than you really do."[14] According to Harris, our children's peer groups, not their parents, determine what kind of people they will grow up to be. She gives an amazing array of evidence ranging from technical research data to anecdotal testimony, all arguing persuasively that this is the case.

At first glance, the notion that parents have little influence on their kids' character seems contrary to everything we believe about parenting. But those who read the book may find Harris's theory more than plausible—even convincing.

Still, a moment's reflection will reveal *why* parents in our culture have less influence on their kids than peer groups do: Most parents have simply abdicated the parental role. They have turned their kids over to their peers. They have invested less time in teaching their kids than the amount of time they have permitted the kids to watch television. They have permitted all their children's spiritual, moral, and ethical instruction to come from television, movies, music, and other children. Even in the best cases, parents rely too much on school teachers, Sunday-school teachers, and youth leaders—all outside the purview of the family. Parents must realize that character is neither inbred by genetics nor picked up by osmosis. Children are *taught* to be what they become. If they have become something other than what the parents hoped for, it is usually because they have simply learned from those who were there to teach them in their parents' absence.

In other words, the parents, not the kids—and not even the peer groups—are ultimately to blame for the parents' diminishing influence in our culture. Whenever outside influences shape a child's character more than the parents, the parents have failed in their duties. It is as simple as that.

Christian parents today desperately need to own this simple principle. Before the throne of God *we* will be held accountable if we have turned our children over to other influences that shape their character in ungodly ways. God has placed in *our* hands the responsibility of bringing our children up in the nurture and admonition of the Lord, and we will give account to God for our stewardship of this great gift. If others have more influence on our children than we, we are *culpable,* not excusable, on those grounds.

God has made parenting a full-time responsibility. There are no coffee breaks from our parental duties. This principle was even built into the Law at Sinai. God prefaced His instructions to the Israelites with this solemn charge: "These words, which I am commanding you today, shall be on your heart. You shall teach them diligently to your children, and shall talk of them when you sit in your house, when you walk by the way, when you lie down, and when you rise up" (Deuteronomy 6:6–7).

That is God's own definition of the parents' task. It means parenting is a full-time assignment in every sense of the expression. No phase of life is exempt. Not one hour of the day is excluded. There is no time-out for the parent who wants to be faithful to this calling.

Some parents think they can compartmentalize their child's life, assign a set number of hours per week to spend on parenting, and then fulfill their duties as parents by making sure the hours they put into the task are "quality time." That whole philosophy is contrary to the spirit of Deuteronomy 6:7, and it is a sure way to guarantee that outside influences will have more influence than the parents in shaping the child's character.

The history of Old Testament Israel is an object lesson about the dangers of neglecting this vital principle. Israel failed miserably when it came to the duty of teaching their children about God's righteousness. Consider this telling verse about the generation of Israelites who first entered the Promised Land. And note that this was merely one generation after God had first given the Law at Sinai: "The people served the LORD all the days of Joshua, and all the days of the elders who outlived Joshua, who had seen all the great works of the LORD which He had done for Israel. . . . When all that generation had been gathered to their fathers, another generation arose after them who did not know the LORD nor the work which He had done for Israel" (Judges 2:7, 10).

In other words, that whole generation of Israelites failed in their responsibility. They neglected to teach their children about the things God had done for Israel. And as a consequence, the next generation turned away from the Lord *en masse:* "Then the children of Israel did evil in the sight of the LORD, and served the Baals; and they forsook the LORD God of their fathers, who had brought them out of the land of Egypt; and they followed other gods from among the gods of the people who were all around them, and they bowed down to them; and they provoked the LORD to anger. They forsook the LORD and served Baal and the Ashtoreths" (vv. 11–13).

The children turned to the evil gods of the Canaanites. Their environment influenced them more than their parents did because the parents abdicated the parental role. The result was idolatry, chaos, and destruction. "Everyone did what was right in his own eyes" (21:25).

The same pattern was repeated again and again throughout Israel's history. Whenever a generation of parents neglected to plant the seeds that would provide shade trees for subsequent generations, the children suffered the spiritual famine that inevitably followed.

The same thing is still occurring to this day. Right now the outlook for the next generation is as bleak as it has ever been. And there will be no turnaround unless this generation of Christian parents resumes the full-time work of planting spiritual shade trees.

For many parents, the first step toward getting back on track must be a fresh commitment to the things of God for themselves. If our own priorities in life are askew, there's no hope of teaching our children what they need to learn.

Parents, take inventory in your own hearts. Do you thirst for God as the deer pants after the water? Or is your own life sending your children a message of hypocrisy and spiritual indifference? Is your own commitment to Christ what you hope to see in your children's lives? Is your obedience to His Word the same kind of submission you long to see from your own kids? These are crucial questions each parent must face if we really want to be successful parents and good role models for our children. Parents who are lax in these areas virtually guarantee that their sons and daughters will fail spiritually. For parents to be derelict in their own spiritual lives is tantamount to cutting down all the shade trees for the next generation in their family.

In the chapters that follow we will examine in closer detail the biblical commandments for parents, for husbands, for wives, and for children. The divine principles for successful Christian parenting will emerge with great clarity. Before you read on, however, I urge you to examine your heart before God, and take a thorough spiritual inventory of how well you are doing, not merely as a parent, but as a child of God.

Two

Understanding Your Child's Greatest Need

Behold, I was brought forth in iniquity,
and in sin my mother conceived me.

—PSALM 51:5

TWO

❦

Understanding Your Child's Greatest Need

Parents tend to make parenting more complex, and yet more superficial, than it really is. Christian parents today are begging for more detailed programs, step-by-step methodologies, and meticulously delineated instructions. Parenting gurus happily oblige. They offer detailed plans for feeding infants *God's way; Christian* methods for toilet-training toddlers; extensive lists of dos and don'ts governing preschoolers' social lives; and similar catalogs of rules for every stage of life up to marriage.

Not all their advice is bad, of course. Some of it can be helpful and even profitable. But compared with the principles for parenting actually set forth in Scripture, most of the so-called "Christian" programs are needlessly complex and sometimes not altogether realistic. Far from being distinctively Christian, some of the advice dispensed in these programs is actually extrabiblical and therefore could safely be ignored. Some of it is simply *bad* advice. For example, I know a young couple who refuse to allow anyone (including Grandma), to rock their baby, *ever.* They were taught in a Christian parenting program that rocking infants to sleep makes them not want to go to bed when they are older. So these parents live in fear that if anyone rocks their baby to sleep, it will awaken some rebellious or self-centered tendency in him that will bear evil fruit when he is older.

Sometimes it seems as if part of the Christian parenting industry thrives by feeding parents' fears that if they do any little thing wrong with their kids, they might seriously damage the child forever, *causing* his character or conduct to be evil. By fueling such concerns, they persuade parents to march lock-step with the program, sign up for seminars year after year, and become utterly dependent on the parenting guru—unable and unwilling to think for themselves. They begin to regard parenting as a mine field strewn with hazards—one wrong step and you risk emotional and psychological damage to your child for life. So they become utterly dependent on systems that map out their every step, and they refuse to deviate from the plan, including those aspects of the program that have no basis in Scripture. Often they even are willing to defy both common sense and parental intuition for the sake of following someone's program. This is not a healthy trend.

As noted in the previous chapter, parenting is supposed to be a joy, not a burden. Scripture repeatedly stresses the blessings of having children and the rich rewards of parenting. "Children are a heritage from the LORD, the fruit of the womb is a reward" (Psalm 127:3). Scripture never portrays parenting as an obstacle course beset with potentially deadly pitfalls.

There is, however, one gigantic pitfall that is too often overlooked by Christian parents. It is something so basic to what we believe as Christians, so clearly taught in Scripture, that no Christian parent should ever be caught off guard by it. Yet I am constantly amazed at how little is said in most Christian parenting curricula about it.

I'm speaking of the child's inborn inclination toward evil.

RECOGNIZING YOUR CHILD'S TRUE POTENTIAL

Every child comes into the world with an insatiable capacity for evil. Even before birth, the human heart is already programmed for sin and selfishness. Humanity's relentless penchant for every kind of depravity is such that, given free reign, every baby has the potential to become a monster.

If you're looking for a theological category for this doctrine, it is normally called "total depravity." It means children do not come into the world seeking God and righteousness. They do not even come into the world with a neutral innocence. They come into the world seeking the fulfillment of sinful and selfish desires. Although the outworking of the sin nature does not necessarily attain full expression in every person's behavior, it is nonetheless called *total* depravity because there is no aspect of the human personality, character, mind, emotions, or will that is free from the corruption of sin or immune to sin's enticements.

Where do children get this depravity? It's not a learned behavior. It is an inbred disposition. Kids get it from their parents, who got it from their parents, who got it from their parents, and so on, all the way back to Adam. Adam "begot a son in his own likeness, after his image" (Genesis 5:3). Adam's children all bore the stamp of sin. They were infected with evil desires. They were born with sinful tastes and an aversion to the things of God—the same aversion that made Adam and Eve try to hide from the Lord's presence (Genesis 3:8). And Adam's children bequeathed the same sin nature to their own progeny. Thus the legacy of corruption and guilt has been handed down to every subsequent generation.

In other words, Adam's fall tainted the entire human race with sin. Both the guilt and the corruption of sin are universal. The apostle Paul wrote, "Through one man sin entered the world, and death through sin, and thus death spread to *all* men, because all sinned" (Romans 5:12, emphasis added). "Through one man's offense judgment came to all men" (v. 18), meaning we inherited the *guilt* of sin. And "by one man's disobedience many were made sinners" (v. 19), meaning we inherited the *corruption* of sin. No one is exempt. No one is born truly innocent. Except for Christ, supernaturally conceived by the Holy Spirit, no person conceived has ever been free from the moral taint of Adam's sin.

Even David, described in Scripture as a man after God's own heart (Acts 13:22), wrote, "I was brought forth in iniquity, and in sin my mother conceived me" (Psalm 51:5). David did not mean his mother conceived him through an act of fornication. He was not suggesting that there is anything sinful about the process by which infants are conceived, for Scripture says, "Marriage is honorable among all, and the bed undefiled" (Hebrews 13:4). The marriage union itself is holy. But when David said he was conceived in sin, he meant his own nature was defiled with sinful tendencies and evil desires from the very moment of his conception.

That is true of all of us. We inherit both the guilt and the corruption of Adam's sin, and we pass it on to our offspring. This is the doctrine of *original sin*. We are born into a fallen race. We inherit a fallen nature. We are inexorably drawn to the lure of sin. We have an appetite for evil and no natural thirst for God. We ultimately have no power of our own to obey God or resist evil: "Because the carnal mind is enmity against God; for it is not subject to the law of God, nor indeed can be. So then, those who are in the flesh cannot please

God" (Romans 8:7–8). Sin colors our very nature. We are born with a sinful bent. We have a fallen character even before we commit our first deliberate act of sin. In fact, we sin *because* we are sinners. We are not innocent creatures who suddenly *become* sinners when we first sin. We are not bent toward good until exposed to evil. We aren't perfect until ruined by our parents, as some would suggest. We are not even born morally *neutral*. We are born sinners.

All of that is also true of our children. Left to themselves, they *will* pursue a course of sin. And left *entirely* to themselves, there is no evil of which they are incapable. Psalm 58:3 says, "The wicked are estranged from the womb; they go astray as soon as they are born, speaking lies." The apostle Paul quoted a string of Old Testament references in his epistle to the Romans, showing from the Scriptures that there are no exceptions to the doctrine of human depravity: "As it is written: 'There is none righteous, no, not one; there is none who understands; there is none who seeks after God. They have all turned aside; they have together become unprofitable; there is none who does good, no, not one. Their throat is an open tomb; with their tongues they have practiced deceit; the poison of asps is under their lips; whose mouth is full of cursing and bitterness. Their feet are swift to shed blood; destruction and misery are in their ways; and the way of peace they have not known. There is no fear of God before their eyes'" (Romans 3:10–18).

Parents instinctively recoil from thinking in such terms. What we see in our newborn infants seems the very epitome of chaste, precious, childlike innocence.

But our children are not innocent when they come into the world, except in the sense that they are naïve and inexperienced. All the potential for sin of every kind is already present in their hearts, in seed form. A proclivity toward sin drives their hearts, minds, and wills. And they have no native potential for true holiness or

God-pleasing righteousness. They are totally depraved already, just waiting for that depravity to express itself. Although they have some knowledge of good in their hearts (Romans 2:14–15), they will not and cannot do the good, because they love evil (Jeremiah 17:9; John 3:19).

If you have trouble with this, just recognize that your children are a miniature version of you.

Many parents live in terror that something they do wrong might mar their child's otherwise virtuous character in some irreparable way. They think if something goes wrong in childhood, the child might begin to drift spiritually or wander morally. But the truth is that our children are already marred by sin from the moment they are conceived. The drive to sin is embedded in their very natures. All that is required for the tragic harvest is that children be allowed to give unrestrained expression to those evil desires.

In other words, children do not go bad because of something their parents do. They are born sinful, and that sinfulness manifests itself because of what their parents do *not* do.

Modern society has produced more mass murderers, perverts, pedophiles, rapists, and lifelong criminals per capita than almost any society in recorded history. And the experts invariably probe the question, what happened to them when they were young? What did their parents do to them? Were they in an abusive environment? Were they in some kind of situation where they were severely mistreated? Did their parents, or society, do something to them to cause them to turn evil?

The truth is that such people are not a product of something their parents *did* to them. They are products of what their parents did *not* do to them. In fact, a surprising number of them had no permanent parental influence whatsoever, but were foster children. Most others had parents whose moral influence was simply absent from their lives.

A case in point is the notorious Jeffrey Dahmer. He became a homosexual, necrophilic, cannibalizing mass murderer. Experts everywhere studied his childhood to try to identify some trauma that might explain such a twisted mind. But Dahmer was raised by a doting mother who kept a detailed scrapbook recording his first steps, his first haircut, and his first tooth. By all accounts, Dahmer's childhood was fairly unexceptional. His most traumatic childhood experiences were a hernia operation and the breakup of his parents' marriage. Dahmer himself stated, "When I was a little kid I was just like anybody else." But in his early teens he started feeding a sadistic appetite by torturing animals and doing gruesome experiments with their carcasses. This occurred during a relatively unsupervised adolescence in which, by his own mother's testimony, she tried her best to give him everything his heart desired. Allowed to do pretty much whatever he liked, Dahmer simply gave full expression to his evil desires. He fed his own sinful appetites. Those appetites then demanded fulfillment through increasingly sinister perversions, until almost nothing would satiate Dahmer's desire for wickedness.

Why is our society producing so many psychopaths and degenerates? Why are so many violent crimes now being committed by kids who have not even entered their teen years? Why do so many apparently "normal" families produce delinquent kids? I believe all those phenomena are rooted in the hands-off style so popular among modern parents. Tolerance and passivity define today's approach to parenting. Restraint and correction are deemed too confining for the child's psyche. Self-esteem has superseded self-control. Parents are afraid to correct wrong behavior. They are urged by *experts* to let their children express themselves freely. Too many parents are utterly absent from their own children's sphere of moral influence. The child's nature is simply permitted to take its course, and by the time the parent realizes the utter depravity of the child's heart, things are already on a course for calamity.

The Bible says, "Foolishness is bound up in the heart of a child; the rod of correction will drive it far from him" (Proverbs 22:15). When children are simply permitted to follow the course of their nature, inevitably the result is disaster.

That little newborn, as adorable as he is, is already a reprobate in the making. And if the parents have no commitment to raise that child in the nurture and admonition of the Lord, he will eventually give full expression to his depravity. And in a society increasingly hostile to godliness and growing more and more tolerant of wickedness, it is no wonder that so many kids left to develop according to their own bent are becoming unimaginably evil. The rash of school shootings over the past decade is only the tip of the iceberg. If you want a taste of how evil the dark side of today's youth culture is, just go down to the local record store and browse the music CDs being sold to the youth market. You'll see music glorifying every evil thing from gross sexual perversion to anger, hatred, and rebellion, and from pointless violence to rank Satan worship. And most parents have no clue what their kids are listening to, or how they behave.

It is simply dangerous, especially in a culture like ours, for a parent to back away and permit a child's own nature to determine, in the moral and ethical sense, what he or she becomes. In that scenario, humanly speaking, there can be only one outcome: a life of sin.

BEHAVIORISM IS NO ANSWER

Some readers at this point may assume that the solution I have in mind for dealing with the child's depravity is strict control of the child's behavior combined with stern discipline. That is not the case.

Certainly both manners and discipline are necessary aspects of proper parenting. But teaching our kids manners is no solution to the problem of human depravity. Tacking on punishment for wrongdoing won't solve the problem, either. In fact, parents who concentrate all their energies on correcting external behavior, or staving off *mis*behavior with threats of discipline, may be doing little more than training hypocrites.

I've seen this occur repeatedly. I know Christian parents who think their parenting is successful because they have taught their children to act politely on cue, answer with "Yes, Sir" and "No, Ma'am," and speak to adults when spoken to. But behind the parents' backs, those same kids can be the most ill-behaved, unruly kids in the church, especially when peers, but no authority figures, are present. And the parents seem blissfully unaware of the children's true character. Almost every teacher and youth leader knows the frustration of trying to deal with a problem child whose parents simply refuse to believe *their* child is capable of serious wrongdoing. This is often because the parents have focused exclusively on issues like public behavior, external decorum, and courtesy to other adults, but they have no understanding of the real state of their own child's heart. Often the child is merely conforming to avoid punishment.

Merely enforcing external behavior with the threat of discipline is sheer behaviorism. The good manners produced by such an approach are merely a conditioned response. While that kind of behavior control may appear to work wonders for a time (especially when the parents are nearby), it does not address the problem of depravity, which is a heart problem.

ISOLATIONISM IS NO ANSWER

Many Christian parents think they have fulfilled the parenting task if they build a cocoon around their kids to isolate them from bad influences. They restrict their children's exposure to television, ban popular music from the home, and sometimes even forbid any fraternization with children whose parents may not share their commitment to this kind of isolation.

There is certainly much on television and in other entertainment media from which our kids *should* be shielded. And since the standards are deteriorating so rapidly, it is essential for Christian parents to provide *some* kind of insulation for their kids. It is simply reckless parenting to permit your kids to surf the Web unsupervised, listen to whatever popular music they choose, or watch television and see movies without any parental oversight. Parents who blithely forfeit control over what their kids see and hear in a culture like this are guilty of appalling malfeasance.

But total isolation is not the answer, either. Naiveté is not a trait to be cultivated in our children. Prudishness is foolish immaturity. It leaves our children gullible and vulnerable. The naïve are the easiest targets for the seductive wiles of temptation. Throughout the Book of Proverbs, the naïve ("simple" in many translations) are held up as *negative* examples:

- "How long, O naive ones, will you love being simple-minded?" (Proverbs 1:22)

- "The waywardness of the naive will kill them, and the complacency of fools will destroy them." (1:32)

- "I saw among the naive, and discerned among the youths a young man lacking sense." (7:7)

- "O naive ones, understand prudence; and, O fools, understand wisdom." (8:5)

- "The naive believes everything, but the sensible man considers his steps. . . . The naive inherit foolishness, but the sensible are crowned with knowledge." (14:15, 18)

- "The prudent sees the evil and hides himself, but the naive go on, and are punished for it." (22:3; cf. 27:12; all quotations immediately above are from the NASB)

Please do not misunderstand; there is a kind of holy innocence that we must cultivate not only in our children but also in ourselves. The apostle Paul wrote, "I want you to be wise in what is good, and simple concerning evil" (Romans 16:19). But in that context he was speaking of knowledge that comes from personal experience. This verse came at the end of several chapters of practical instruction from the apostle. He was saying he wanted the Romans to be well-practiced in good behavior, but inexperienced when it came to evil.

Inexperience and naiveté are not the same thing. Paul did not mean he wanted them oblivious to the existence of evil. He was certainly not advocating deliberate ignorance or a willful blindness to the *reality* of evil. He wanted them to be prudent, not prudish. The difference is significant.

Parents cannot—and *should* not—try to isolate their children totally from the truth about sin and the subtleties of temptation. We should not cultivate the kind of "innocence" in our children that leaves them exposed and vulnerable to temptations they never even imagined existed. Our task is to teach them discernment, not raise them to be prudes.

I know of one Christian parenting course that encourages moms and dads to avoid giving their children any kind of detailed instruction whatsoever about sexual matters, not only during childhood and adolescence, but up to and including the son or daughter's wedding night. The child's inevitable questions about anatomy and bodily development during puberty are supposed to be deflected with vague answers, making it clear that the very *topic* of sex is taboo. If questions about reproduction need to be addressed, they should be dealt with using the parts of a flower, for fear that anything more explicit will take away the child's innocence. According to this program, mere exposure to the *facts* about human reproduction jeopardizes your child's moral innocence. This particular course goes as far as cautioning parents not to expose their kids to classical art exhibits because they include statues and paintings that portray nude figures.

That sort of isolationism is a recipe for disaster. It is a wholly unbiblical perspective. Sex is not portrayed in Scripture as inherently evil, nor is it treated as taboo. Sex outside of marriage is certainly sinful, but within marriage, the union of husband and wife is holy and honorable (Hebrews 13:4). The subject per se poses no threat to a proper, godly, moral innocence. How can our children hope to have a proper and biblical understanding of these things if we treat the subject itself as a threat to their innocence? Scripture certainly does not do that. An entire book of the Old Testament— the Song of Solomon—was written to celebrate the joy and the purity of marital intimacy. There is certainly no command or principle in Scripture that would make such matters off limits for parental instruction.

On the contrary, instructing children properly in such matters lies at the heart of the parents' responsibility. Abdicate this responsibility, and you practically insure that your children will be more influenced by the values and mores they learn from schoolteachers and peers. It is nearly impossible, and certainly a wrong-headed approach to parenting, to keep children *totally* isolated from all influences outside the family. So in all likelihood they *will* learn about these things from other sources, no matter how they have been sheltered. If the parents have declined to foster a godly knowledge of sex and human reproduction, the likelihood that the child will develop *ungodly* attitudes toward the subject are multiplied.

Besides, the notion that parents are preserving a child's innocence simply by declaring certain topics taboo and isolating kids from the truth about them ignores the reality that many of our sinful desires are inborn. Sinful appetites are inherent in our fallen nature. They are not merely learned behaviors. Refuse to teach your children *anything* about sex, and you not only forfeit the opportunity to give them a righteous perspective, but you may also set loose the child's own evil imagination to work overtime.

A similar principle holds true for those who attempt to isolate their children from all the negative influences of secular culture. Extreme isolationism costs parents valuable opportunities to teach their kids discernment. For example, it may well be more profitable to watch "Star Wars" with your kids and teach them how to identify and refute its erroneous New Age philosophies, rather than trying to keep your children spiritually quarantined, completely shut off from all such influences.

In the first place, parents will not be able to isolate their children forever. The day will come when they are exposed to the real world, and they had better be prepared with discernment skills and the wisdom to perceive and resist the wiles of the devil and the enticements of the world.

But in the second place, it is simply a mistake to think that shutting our kids off from outside influences will somehow keep them from any temptation to evil. The most persistent source of temptation is not the world or the devil, but the flesh. You can often elude the influence of the world and the devil, but you cannot escape the influence of your own flesh. The flesh is a constant source of temptation from which you *cannot* sequester your children.

It is a grave mistake to think of our children as little angels who need to be handled delicately so they don't get corrupted. Rather, they are corrupt little sinners who need to be led to righteousness.

SELF-ESTEEM IS NO ANSWER

One philosophy that has shaped popular approaches to parenting for decades, both in the secular arena and in the church, is based on the notion that parents should do everything possible to bolster their child's self-esteem. Self-esteem experts tell us that if children and adolescents (not to mention adults) had a higher opinion of themselves, most of their psychological and emotional problems would be solved.

The root of all such problems, they say, is that people don't have enough self-respect. If they had more pride—if they saw themselves as good, noble, wonderful people—they would not only behave better, but they also would treat others better.

Advocates of self-esteem typically target parents, claiming that our parents are most to blame for our low self-esteem and warning parents to do all they can to elevate their own kids' sense of self-love. They caution parents not to focus on correcting misbehavior, but to make a greater effort to bolster the child's self-image. They suggest that children must be taught to love themselves the way they are; to accept themselves; and to feel good about themselves.

The same theme is hammered in every forum from children's books to popular songs. A typical example is Whitney Houston's 1986 double-platinum song, "The Greatest Love of All"—a shameless paean to self-esteem.

Entertainers, educators, and pundits of all types are singing the same chorus, extolling self-love as the great solution to all our kids' troubles. Children's sports leagues have begun sponsoring tournaments in which there are no losers (and consequently no winners, nor any real competition). Schools have adopted various grading systems that insure no one ever fails, virtually eliminating students' incentive to work hard. One new technique for encouraging self-esteem is "inventive spelling." Teachers allow—even encourage—kids to spell words in whatever way "feels right" to them. Spelling is never corrected for fear it will stifle the child's ability to express himself in writing. (I practiced inventive spelling when I was in school, but none of my teachers saw the creative genius in the technique.)

Hard work, true excellence, good behavior, and self-control have all been sacrificed at the altar of self-esteem. Above all, we're told, we must teach our kids to like themselves just the way they are. Suggesting there are things they need to change is deemed the greatest *faux pas* any parent could ever commit. Thus millions of parents have simply abandoned all efforts to spur their kids to greater accomplishments or more noble character.

But the champions of self-esteem don't want parents to feel badly for their parental failures, either. An article on self-esteem in a trendy parenting magazine assures parents they need to learn to love themselves before they can help their kids attain proper self-esteem. One critic of self-esteemism sagely observed that this is one of the cleverest philosophical tropes of the self-esteem movement: self-absorption as altruism. Selfishness has been turned into a virtue—"the greatest love of all."

The truth is that much of the modern effort to spark kids' self-esteem is simply pouring gasoline on a runaway fire. It encourages already selfish kids to think they are justified in wanting their own way. It makes parents think they must defer to the child, no matter what, because the child has a right to express himself freely, so that he feels good about himself. All this only escalates out-of-control behavior and feeds all the worst tendencies of human depravity.

Want to *insure* that your child will become a delinquent? Feed his self-esteem and then compound the problem of selfishness by refusing to correct him when he is wrong.

Self-esteemism is based on an unbiblical perspective. It is diametrically opposed to the truth of human depravity. Moreover, while Scripture commends self-*control* as a fruit of the Spirit, the Bible has nothing positive to say about self-esteem, self-love, or any other variety of self-centeredness. Despite how often we hear the mantra chanted by self-proclaimed experts, self-esteemism is *not* what your child needs.

THE CHILD'S GREATEST NEED: REGENERATION

There's only one remedy for the child's inborn depravity: The new birth—regeneration. As Jesus said to Nicodemus, "That which is born of the flesh is flesh, and that which is born of the Spirit is spirit. . . . [Therefore,] you must be born again" (John 3:6–7).

"Born of the flesh" with a sinful bent, your children have no power to free themselves from sin's bondage. They lack the Holy Spirit. They have no capacity to please God or to obey Him from the heart. Having been born of flesh, they are carnal. And "the carnal mind is enmity against God; for it is not subject to the law of God, nor indeed can be. So then, those who are in the flesh cannot please God" (Romans 8:7–8).

Elsewhere Scripture describes the unregenerate as "dead in trespasses and sins . . . [conducting themselves] in the lusts of [their] flesh, fulfilling the desires of the flesh and of the mind . . . by nature children of wrath" (Ephesians 2:1, 3). Like it or not, that is an apt description of your children—until they are born again.

Your top-priority job as a parent, then, is to be an evangelist in your home. You need to teach your children the law of God; teach them the gospel of divine grace; show them their need for a Savior; and point them to Jesus Christ as the only One who can save them. If they grow up without a keen awareness of their need for salvation, you as a parent will have failed in your primary task as their spiritual leader.

Note this, however: Regeneration is not something you can do *for* them. Parents who force, coerce, or manipulate their kids may pressure them into a *false* profession, but genuine faith is something only divine grace can prompt. The new birth is a work of the Holy Spirit. "The wind blows where it wishes, and you hear the sound of it, but cannot tell where it comes from and where it goes. So is everyone who is born of the Spirit" (John 3:8). God works sovereignly in your children's hearts to draw them to Himself. Their salvation is a matter that must ultimately be settled between them and God.

But as parents, you are nonetheless responsible to exalt Christ in your home and point your kids to Him as Savior. "How shall they believe in Him of whom they have not heard? And how shall they hear without a preacher" (Romans 10:14)? As believing parents, you are the first and most important preachers God has given them. They will observe your lives up close, to see whether *you* seriously believe what you are teaching them. They will weigh what you teach them about these matters from the earliest time they can understand anything. You have a better opportunity than anyone to help frame what they know about Christ. Every moment of their lives is a teaching opportunity (Deuteronomy 6:6–7), and you should use those opportunities to the best advantage for your kids' sake.

Here's why so many parents think of parenting as hopelessly complex: They are ignoring their child's *greatest* need and focusing their energies instead on stoking the child's self-image, managing the child's external behavior, protecting the child from outside influences, or some other approach that deals with symptoms rather than the cause. All such approaches only multiply the complexities of parenting.

It is remarkable that when the apostle Paul outlined the various roles and responsibilities for family members, he summarized the entire parenting task in a one-verse admonition to fathers. Having reminded children of their duty under the Fifth Commandment, he turned his attention to the parents' role: "Do not provoke your children to wrath, but bring them up in the training and admonition of the Lord" (Ephesians 6:4).

We would not be surprised if the apostle Paul took a whole chapter, or even an entire epistle, to outline the responsibilities of parents. Instead, he summarized all of parenting in a single verse, and he was able to do so because the task is so highly defined. "Bring them up in the training and admonition of the Lord."

In a future chapter, we'll look at the negative side of Paul's admonition ("Do not provoke your children to wrath"). But in the chapter that immediately follows, we'll begin examining what it means to bring up our children in the nurture and admonition of the Lord. And we'll start with some very practical guidelines for addressing your children's greatest need—leading them to Christ.

T HREE

Good News for Your Kids

*Assuredly, I say to you, whoever does not receive the kingdom
of God as a little child will by no means enter it.*

— MARK 10:15

THREE

Good News for Your Kids

The one practical question I am most commonly asked by parents is this: How should I present the gospel to my children? Pitfalls, both real and imagined, intimidate virtually every parent who contemplates this responsibility. On one hand, there's the danger of oversimplification. On the other hand, we don't want to confound our kids with theological details that are over their heads. What's the best approach to take? When is the best time to start? How old is "old enough" for our kids to have genuine saving faith? What if they ask questions we cannot answer? How do we know we're doing it right? It seems all too easy for parents to give their kids an inadequate or twisted message.

But there's no need to be paralyzed by such fears. The gospel is simple and should be presented simply. Parents have the best years of the child's life to explain, clarify, stress, and reemphasize gospel truths. The key is to be faithful and consistent in both teaching and exemplifying the gospel. One of the worst things parents can do is be intimidated into thinking someone else would make a better evangelist for their child, thus abdicating their most crucial responsibility, missing the best opportunities for reaching their children, and forfeiting the best blessings of parenthood.

TAKE YOUR TIME AND BE THOROUGH

Here's some foundational advice: Think of leading your children to Christ as a long-term, full-time assignment—the most important duty God has given you as a parent.

Be thorough. There is no good reason for parents to soften or abridge the gospel for their kids. Parents more than anyone have ample time to be thorough and clear; to explain and illustrate; to listen to feedback; to correct misunderstanding; and to clarify and review the difficult parts. It is the best possible scenario for evangelism. The wise parent will be faithful, patient, persistent, and thorough. In fact, that is precisely what Scripture demands of every parent: "These words, which I am commanding you today, shall be on your heart. You shall teach them diligently to your children, and shall talk of them when you sit in your house, when you walk by the way, when you lie down, and when you rise up" (Deuteronomy 6:6–7).

Don't think of the gospel as something suited only for special evangelistic occasions. Don't assume Sunday school classes or children's Bible clubs will give your children all the gospel truth they need. Look for and seize the many daily opportunities you will have for highlighting and punctuating gospel truth in your kids' thinking.

Don't rely too much on canned or formulaic gospel presentations. Many of the programmed approaches to child evangelism leave out key parts of the message. They fail to explain the concepts of sin and the holiness of God. They say nothing of repentance. But then they typically solicit some active response from the child—

a show of hands in a group setting, a rote prayer on Mother's lap, or almost anything that may be counted as a positive response. After that, the child is deemed regenerate, and the parents are encouraged to focus on giving verbal assurances of salvation. As a consequence, the church is filled with teenagers and adults whose hearts are devoid of real love for Christ, but who think they are genuine Christians because of something they *did* as children.

Avoid that pitfall. Do not assume your child's first positive response is full-fledged saving faith. If you think a three-year-old's prayer inviting Jesus into her heart automatically guarantees her a place in the kingdom, your notion of what it means to trust Christ isn't very biblical.

It is true that saving faith is a childlike trust, and in that sense all sinners must become like little children in order to be saved (Matthew 18:3–4). But the emphasis in that statement is not on the *ignorance* of children but on their lack of achievement and their utter helplessness. They have no personal accomplishments worth anything in saving them (Philippians 3:7–9). They are helpless, depending totally on God to provide everything for them. Just like an infant.

On the other hand, real faith involves understanding and affirming some important concepts that may be out of reach for small children (Romans 10:14; cf. 1 Corinthians 14:20). The sole object of genuine faith is Jesus Christ *as He is presented to us in the gospel.* How can children exercise true saving faith before they are old enough to understand and affirm essential, objective elements of gospel truth? Saving faith is not *blind* faith. Real saving faith cannot be ignorant of essential gospel concepts such as good and evil, sin and punishment, repentance and faith, God's holiness and His wrath against sin, Christ as God incarnate, the idea of atonement for sin and the meaning of the resurrection and lordship of Christ.

The specific age at which the child's understanding is mature enough to grasp such concepts may differ for each child. (So there's no reliable way to pinpoint a physical "age of accountability.") But until the child demonstrates some degree of real understanding and some measure of spiritual fruit, parents should not be quick to regard the child's regeneration as a settled matter.

Nonetheless, don't write off childlike expressions of faith as meaningless or trivial. Parents should encourage every sign of faith in their children. Don't ridicule or belittle them for the things they fail to understand. Use the opportunity to teach them more. Feed their desire to learn about Christ, and encourage their every profession of faith. Even if you conclude it's too early to regard their interest in Christ as mature faith, don't deride it as merely a false profession. It may be the seed from which mature faith will later emerge. And don't be discouraged by misunderstanding or ignorance. Even the most mature believer does not fully comprehend all truth accurately. Keep teaching them in the spirit of Deuteronomy 6:6–7.

Nothing a parent can do will actually guarantee the salvation of a child. We cannot believe *for* them by proxy. We might coerce or manipulate them into a spurious profession of faith, but *genuine* faith is prompted by God's work in the child's heart (John 6:44–45). We might talk them into a false assurance, but *true* assurance is the Holy Spirit's work (Romans 8:15–16). Be careful not to intrude into a realm that belongs to God alone. Don't employ external inducements, peer pressure, the power of suggestion, the lure of approval, the fear of rejection, or any other artificial means, to entice a superficial response from your child. But be faithful, patient, and thorough. And bathe your efforts in prayer for your children's salvation, always bearing in mind that God does His work where you cannot—in the child's heart.

TEACH THEM THE WHOLE COUNSEL OF GOD

Exactly how should we present the gospel to our children? Many who ask this question are seeking a simplified outline. They want a capsulized plan of salvation where the message is distilled in four or five basic points, or fewer if possible. Modern evangelicalism is frankly too prone to this kind of gospel reductionism. The lineup in one church's tract rack included all these titles: *Six Steps to Peace With God; Five Things God Wants You to Know; Four Spiritual Laws; Three Truths You Can't Live Without; Two Issues You Must Settle;* and *One Way to Heaven.*

As I noted earlier, many of the packaged-formula approaches to the gospel deliberately omit important truths like repentance and God's wrath against sin. Some influential voices in modern evangelicalism have actually argued that those truths (and others, including Christ's lordship, His call to surrender, and the high cost of discipleship) are extraneous to the gospel. They say such matters should not even be brought up when talking to unbelievers. Other Christian leaders, desiring ecumenical unity among Catholics, Orthodox, and evangelicals, suggest that important doctrinal issues such as justification by faith and substitutionary atonement are not really essential to the gospel. They're in effect also calling for a bare-bones approach to the gospel. Their ecumenical openness implies that virtually any kind of generic faith in Christ may be regarded as authentic saving faith, ignoring the fact that the New Testament condemns those who profess to believe in Christ while rejecting or twisting the doctrine of justification (Galatians 1:6–9). It seems *many* evangelicals are obsessed with finding out how little of God's truth a person can believe and still get to heaven. Many of the modern popular approaches to evangelism have been shaped accordingly.

But parents more than anyone should resist the temptation to think in such terms. The sort of constant, faithful, diligent teaching required by Deuteronomy 6:6–7 is incompatible with a minimalist approach to the gospel.

The gospel is the good news about Christ. There is a sense in which the gospel includes *all* truth about Him. There's no need to think of any aspect of biblical truth as incompatible with or extraneous to the gospel. In fact, since Christ is the sum and the summit of all biblical revelation (Hebrews 1:1–3), every truth in Scripture ultimately points to Him. And therefore none of it is out of place in evangelistic contexts. One could accurately say, then, that parents who want to be thorough in evangelizing their children need to teach them *the whole counsel of God,* taking care to show the gospel ramifications in all that truth. That, I believe, is the true spirit of what Deuteronomy 6:6–7 calls for.

No single formula can possibly meet the needs of every unregenerate person anyway. Those who are *ignorant* need to be told who Christ is and why He offers the only hope of salvation (Romans 10:3). Those who are *careless* need to be confronted with the reality of impending judgment (John 16:11). Those who are *fearful* need to hear that God is merciful, delighting not in the death of the wicked but pleading with sinners to come to Him for mercy (Ezekiel 33:11). Those who are *hostile* need to be shown the futility of opposing the will of God (Psalm 2:1–4). Those who are *self-righteous* need to have their sin exposed by the demands of God's law (Romans 3:20). Those who are *proud* need to hear that God hates pride (1 Peter 5:5). *All* sinners must understand that God is holy and that Christ has met the demands of God's perfect righteousness on behalf of sinners (1 Corinthians 1:30). Every gospel presentation should include an explanation of Christ's sacrificial death for sin (15:3). And the message is not the gospel if it does not also recount His burial and the triumph of His resurrection (vv. 4, 17).

HIGHLIGHT THE DOCTRINES
MOST CRUCIAL TO THE GOSPEL

Along with a commitment to be thorough, however, parents must also take great care to highlight certain truths that are particularly crucial to a correct understanding of the gospel. Here are some pointers that will help keep you on course:[1]

Teach them about God's holiness

"The fear of the Lord is the beginning of wisdom" (Psalm 111:10, Job 28:28; Proverbs 1:7; 9:10; 15:33; Ecclesiastes 12:13; Micah 6:9). That is not speaking of a craven fear. It is not the kind of fear that regards God as capricious in His anger. Rather, it is a devout, reverential fear of offending God's holiness, based on a true understanding of God as One who is "of purer eyes than to behold evil, and [One who] cannot look on wickedness" (Habakkuk 1:13).

God is utterly holy, and His law therefore demands perfect holiness. "'For I am the LORD your God. You shall therefore consecrate yourselves, and you shall be holy; for I am holy. Neither shall you defile yourselves. . . . You shall therefore be holy, for I am holy" (Leviticus 11:44–45). "He is a holy God. He is a jealous God; He will not [merely overlook] your transgressions nor your sins" (Joshua 24:19). "No one is holy like the LORD, for there is none besides You, nor is there any rock like our God" (1 Samuel 2:2). "Who is able to stand before this holy LORD God" (6:20)? The LORD is in His holy temple, the LORD's throne is in heaven; His eyes behold, His eyelids test the sons of men. The LORD tests the righteous, but the wicked and the one who loves violence His soul hates. Upon the wicked He will rain coals; fire and brimstone and a burning wind shall be the portion of their cup. For the LORD is righteous, He loves righteousness; His countenance beholds the upright (Psalm 11:4–7). "Be holy, for I am holy" (1 Peter 1:16). "Without [holiness] no one will see the Lord" (Hebrews 12:14).

Because He is holy, God hates sin. "You shall not bow down to [false gods] nor serve them. For I, the LORD your God, am a jealous God, visiting the iniquity of the fathers on the children to the third and fourth generations of those who hate Me" (Exodus 20:5). "You are not a God who takes pleasure in wickedness, nor shall evil dwell with You" (Psalm 5:4). "God is a just judge, and God is angry with the wicked every day" (7:11).

Sinners cannot stand before Him. "The ungodly shall not stand in the judgment, nor sinners in the congregation of the righteous" (Psalm 1:5). "The boastful shall not stand in Your sight; You hate all workers of iniquity" (5:5). "Who may ascend into the hill of the LORD? Or who may stand in His holy place? He who has clean hands and a pure heart, who has not lifted up his soul to an idol, nor sworn deceitfully" (24:3–4).

Show them their sin

Be sure to teach your children from the youngest age that misbehavior is not merely an offense against Mom and Dad; it's also a sin against a holy God, who demands that children obey their parents (Exodus 20:12).

Help educate your children's conscience so that they view their own misbehavior as a sin for which they will eventually answer to God—not merely misconduct against their parents. Teach them this with love and genuine compassion, not in a browbeating manner.

Helping your children understand their own sin does not mean constantly criticizing them and running them down. It certainly doesn't mean you refuse to commend them when they do well. I heard about one set of parents who got very upset with Grandma, who while bouncing their smiling six-month-old on her knee said to the infant, "What a good boy!" These parents snatched the baby away and sternly reprimanded the grandparent, accusing her of teaching the infant "false doctrine." That's more than a little excessive.

Teaching them they are sinners does not mean belittling them or tormenting them with constant verbal battering about their failures. The goal is not to trample their spirit by continually berating them. Instead, you need to instruct them tenderly and help them view their own fallenness from God's perspective. They need to appreciate *why* they are drawn to sin, and ultimately they must sense their own need of redemption.

Jesus said, "Those who are well have no need of a physician, but those who are sick. I did not come to call the righteous, but sinners, to repentance" (Mark 2:17).

Don't be afraid to teach your children what God's law demands. Law and gospel have differing purposes, of course. We know that sinners cannot be justified by the works of the law (Galatians 2:16). But don't conclude that the law therefore plays no role whatsoever in the proclamation of the gospel. The law reveals our sin (Romans 3:20; 7:7) and shows the real nature of sin for what it is (7:13). The law is a tutor to lead us to Christ (Galatians 3:24). It is the chief means God uses to make sinners see their own helplessness. Far from being out of place in gospel instruction, the law and its righteous demands marked the starting point of the apostle Paul's systematic gospel presentation (Romans 1:16–3:20). The law's moral standards give us the necessary foundation for understanding what sin is.

Sin is violation of God's law. "Whosoever committeth sin transgresseth also the law: for sin is the transgression of the law" ɔhn 3:4, KJV). "All unrighteousness is sin" (5:17). "I would not have known sin except through the law" (Romans 7:7).

Sin is what makes true peace impossible for unbelievers. "The wicked are like the troubled sea, when it cannot rest, whose waters cast up mire and dirt. 'There is no peace,' says my God, 'for the wicked'" (Isaiah 57:20–21). "Woe to those who devise iniquity" (Micah 2:1).

All have sinned. "All have sinned and fall short of the glory of God" (Romans 3:23).

"As it is written: 'There is none righteous, no, not one; there is none who understands; there is none who seeks after God. They have all turned aside; they have together become unprofitable; there is none who does good, no, not one' " (3:10–12).

Sin makes the sinner worthy of death. "The soul who sins shall die" (Ezekiel 18:4). "Sin, when it is full-grown, brings forth death" (James 1:15). "For the wages of sin is death" (Romans 6:23).

Sinners can do nothing to earn salvation. "We are all like an unclean thing, and all our righteousnesses are like filthy rags; we all fade as a leaf, and our iniquities, like the wind, have taken us away" (Isaiah 64:6). "By the deeds of the law no flesh will be justified in His sight" (Romans 3:20). "A man is not justified by the works of the law . . . for by the works of the law no flesh shall be justified" (Galatians 2:16).

Sinners cannot change their own sin nature. " 'Though you wash yourself with lye, and use much soap, yet your iniquity is marked before Me,' says the LORD God" (Jeremiah 2:22). "Can the Ethiopian change his skin or the leopard its spots? Then may you also do good who are accustomed to do evil" (13:23). "The carnal mind is enmity against God; for it is not subject to the law of God, nor indeed can be. So then, those who are in the flesh cannot please God" (Romans 8:7–8).

Sinners are therefore in a helpless state. "It is appointed for men to die once, but after this the judgment" (Hebrews 9:27). "There is nothing covered that will not be revealed, nor hidden that will not be known. Therefore whatever you have spoken in the dark will be heard in the light, and what you have spoken in the ear in inner rooms will be proclaimed on the housetops" (Luke 12:2–3). "God will judge the secrets of men by Jesus Christ" (Romans 2:16). "The cowardly, unbelieving, abominable, murderers, sexually immoral, sorcerers, idolaters, and all liars shall have their part in the lake which burns with fire and brimstone, which is the second death" (Revelation 21:8).

Instruct them about Christ and what He has done

Teaching your children about their own sin is by no means an end in itself. You must also point them to the only remedy for sin—Jesus Christ. He is the heart of the gospel message, so instructing them about Jesus Christ should be the ultimate focus and the design of *all* your spiritual instruction.

He is eternally God. "In the beginning was the Word, and the Word was with God, and the Word was God. He was in the beginning with God. All things were made through Him, and without Him nothing was made that was made. . . . And the Word became flesh and dwelt among us, and we beheld His glory, the glory as of the only begotten of the Father, full of grace and truth" (John 1:1–3, 14). "In Him dwells all the fullness of the Godhead bodily" (Colossians 2:9).

He is Lord of all. "He is Lord of lords and King of kings" (Revelation 17:14). "God also has highly exalted Him and given Him the name which is above every name, that at the name of Jesus every knee should bow, of those in heaven, and of those on earth, and of those under the earth, and that every tongue should confess that Jesus Christ is Lord, to the glory of God the Father" (Philippians 2:9–11). "He is Lord of all" (Acts 10:36).

He became man. "Being in the form of God, did not consider it [a thing to be held on to] to be equal with God, but made Himself of no reputation, taking the form of a bondservant, and coming in the likeness of men" (Philippians 2:6–7).

He is utterly pure and sinless. "[He] was in all points tempted as we are, yet without sin" (Hebrews 4:15). He "committed no sin, nor was deceit found in His mouth"; who, when He was reviled, did not revile in return; when He suffered, He did not threaten, but committed Himself to Him who judges righteously" (1 Peter 2:22–23). "He was manifested to take away our sins, and in Him there is no sin" (1 John 3:5).

The sinless one became a sacrifice for our sin. "He made Him who knew no sin to be sin for us, that we might become the righteousness of God in Him" (2 Corinthians 5:21). He "gave Himself for us, that He might redeem us from every lawless deed and purify for Himself His own special people, zealous for good works" (Titus 2:14).

He shed His own blood as an atonement for sin. "In Him we have redemption through His blood, the forgiveness of sins, according to the riches of His grace" (Ephesians 1:7). "[He] loved us and washed us from our sins in His own blood" (Revelation 1:5).

He died on the cross to provide a way of salvation for sinners. "He Himself bore our sins in His body on the cross, that we might die to sin and live to righteousness; for by His wounds you were healed" (1 Peter 2:24, NASB). "It pleased the Father . . . by Him to reconcile all things to Himself, by Him, whether things on earth or things in heaven, having made peace through the blood of His cross" (Colossians 1:20).

He rose triumphantly from the dead. Christ was "declared to be the Son of God with power according to the Spirit of holiness, by the resurrection from the dead" (Romans 1:4). "[He] was delivered up because of our offenses, and was raised because of our justification" (4:25). "I delivered to you first of all that which I also received: that Christ died for our sins according to the Scriptures, and that He was buried, and that He rose again the third day according to the Scriptures" (1 Corinthians 15:3–4).

His righteousness is imputed to those who trust Him. "You are in Christ Jesus, who became for us . . . righteousness" (1 Corinthians 1:30). ". . . That we might become the righteousness of God in Him" (2 Corinthians 5:21). "To him who does not work but believes on Him who justifies the ungodly, his faith is accounted for righteousness . . . God imputes righteousness apart from works" (Romans 4:5–6). "Yet indeed I also count all things loss for the excellence of the knowledge of Christ Jesus my Lord, for whom I have suffered the loss of all things, and count them as rubbish, that I may gain Christ and be found in Him, not having my own righteousness, which is from the law, but that which is through faith in Christ, the righteousness which is from God by faith" (Philippians 3:8–9).

Thus He freely justifies all who trust in Him. "[We are] justified freely by His grace through the redemption that is in Christ Jesus" (Romans 3:24). "Therefore, having been justified by faith, we have peace with God through our Lord Jesus Christ, through whom also we have access by faith into this grace in which we stand, and rejoice in hope of the glory of God" (5:1–2). "Having now been justified by His blood, we shall be saved from wrath through Him" (v. 9). "A man is not justified by the works of the law but by faith in Jesus Christ" (Galatians 2:16). ""Most assuredly, I say to you, he who hears My word and believes in Him who sent Me has everlasting life, and shall not come into judgment, but has passed from death into life" (John 5:24).

Tell them what God demands of sinners

God calls sinners to repentance (Acts 17:30). Genuine repentance is not self-reformation or the turning over of a new leaf. It is a turning of the heart to God from all that is evil.

It's helpful to stress that repentance is a heart-turning and should not be equated with any external action on the child's part. In many modern evangelicals' minds, the act of praying to invite Jesus into the heart has become practically a sacramental means of salvation. The same thing is true of lifting a hand in a meeting, or coming forward to the altar. But such external actions have no intrinsic saving efficacy. They are all works, and works cannot save. *Faith*—a repentant trust in Christ alone for salvation—is the one true instrument of our justification, according to Scripture. "For by grace you have been saved through faith, and that not of yourselves; it is the gift of God, not of works, lest anyone should boast" (Ephesians 2:8–9).

If you use metaphors to clarify aspects of the gospel for children, be sure to distinguish carefully between metaphor and reality. When we use vivid imagery, such as describing sinful hearts dark or dirty with sin, or when we encourage kids to think of Jesus knocking at the door of their hearts, they tend to form a very literal picture in their minds. Such word pictures, if not carefully explained, can actually be an impediment, rather than an aid, to understanding the gospel.[2] If the child comes away thinking in literal terms that Jesus is standing at the heart's door, awaiting an invitation to take up residency, we have failed to make the gospel clear.

It's best to avoid all such empasis on external actions, and keep focusing instead on the response Scripture calls for from sinners.

Repent. "I have no pleasure in the death of one who dies," says the Lord God. 'Therefore turn and live'" (Ezekiel 18:32)! "Repent therefore and be converted, that your sins may be blotted out" (Acts 3:19). "God . . . commands all men everywhere to repent" (17:30). "Repent, turn to God, and do works befitting repentance" (26:20). That verse speaks not of *meritorious* works, but it indicates that the inevitable fruit of true repentance is a changed life (cf. Matthew 3:7–8).

Turn your heart from all that dishonors God. "[Turn] to God from idols to serve the living and true God" (1 Thessalonians 1:9). "Repent, turn away from your idols, and turn your faces away from all your abominations" (Ezekiel 14:6). "Repent, and turn from all your transgressions, so that iniquity will not be your ruin" (18:30). "Let the wicked forsake his way, and the unrighteous man his thoughts; let him return to the Lord" (Isaiah 55:7).

Follow Jesus. "If anyone desires to come after Me, let him deny himself, and take up his cross daily, and follow Me" (Luke 9:23). "No one, having put his hand to the plow, and looking back, is fit for the kingdom of God" (v. 62). "If anyone serves Me, let him follow Me; and where I am, there My servant will be also. If anyone serves Me, him My Father will honor" (John 12:26). "You are My friends if you do whatever I command you" (John 15:14).

Trust Him as Lord and Savior. "Believe on the Lord Jesus Christ, and you will be saved" (Acts 16:31). "If you confess with your mouth the Lord Jesus and believe in your heart that God has raised Him from the dead, you will be saved" (Romans 10:9).

Advise them to count the cost thoughtfully

Don't downplay the hard demands of Christ. Don't portray the Christian life as a life of ease, free from difficulties and dilemmas. Keep reminding your kids that the true price of following Christ always involves sacrifice, and the prelude to glory is suffering. It's true that

Christ offers the water of life freely to all who will take it (Revelation 22:17). But those who do are making unconditional commitment to follow Him that may literally cost them their very lives.

Here is why all the central truths of the gospel focus on the cross: It reveals how heinous our sin is. It shows the intensity of God's wrath against sin. It reveals the great love of God in paying such a high price for redemption. But it also serves as a fitting metaphor for the cost of following Christ. Jesus himself spoke repeatedly of the cross in those terms.

A. W. Tozer wrote,

> The cross . . . always has its way. It wins by defeating its opponent and imposing its will upon him. It always dominates. It never compromises, never dickers nor confers, never surrenders a point for the sake of peace. It cares not for peace; it cares only to end its opposition as fast as possible.
>
> With perfect knowledge of all this, Christ said, "If any man will come after me, let him deny himself, and take up his cross, and follow me." So the cross not only brings Christ's life to an end, it ends also the first life, the old life, of every one of His true followers. It destroys the old pattern, the Adam pattern, in the believer's life, and brings it to an end. Then the God who raised Christ from the dead raises the believer and a new life begins.
>
> This, and nothing less, is true Christianity. . . .
>
> We must do something about the cross, and one of two things only we can do—flee it or die upon it.[3]

Jesus repeatedly stated that the cost of following Him involves a willingness to sacrifice all.

Take up your cross. "Come, take up the cross, and follow Me" (Mark 10:21). "Whoever desires to come after Me, let him deny himself, and take up his cross, and follow Me. For whoever desires to save his life will lose it, but whoever loses his life for My sake and the gospel's will save it. For what will it profit a man if he gains the whole world, and loses his own soul? Or what will a man give in exchange for his soul" (Mark 8:34–37)?

Be prepared to follow Christ even to death. "Most assuredly, I say to you, unless a grain of wheat falls into the ground and dies, it remains alone; but if it dies, it produces much grain. He who loves his life will lose it, and he who hates his life in this world will keep it for eternal life" (John 12:24–25).

If anyone comes to Me and does not hate his father and mother, wife and children, brothers and sisters, yes, and his own life also, he cannot be My disciple. And whoever does not bear his cross and come after Me cannot be My disciple. For which of you, intending to build a tower, does not sit down first and count the cost, whether he has enough to finish it; lest, after he has laid the foundation, and is not able to finish, all who see it begin to mock him, saying, "This man began to build and was not able to finish." Or what king, going to make war against another king, does not sit down first and consider whether he is able with ten thousand to meet him who comes against him with twenty thousand? Or else, while the other is still a great way off, he sends a delegation and asks conditions of peace. So likewise, whoever of you does not forsake all that he has cannot be My disciple (Luke 14:26–33).

Do not think that I came to bring peace on earth. I did not come to bring peace but a sword. For I have come to "set a man against his father, a daughter against her mother, and a daughter-in-law against her mother-in-law"; and "a man's enemies will be those of his own household." He who loves father or mother more than Me is not worthy of Me. And he who loves son or daughter more than Me is not worthy of Me. And he who does not take his cross and follow after Me is not worthy of Me (Matthew 10:34–38).

Urge them to trust Christ

We began by noting that regeneration is the Holy Spirit's work in the heart, and we cautioned parents not to employ artificial means or external pressure to coax a shallow profession of faith from the child. Nonetheless, there is an urgency inherent in the gospel message itself, and it is right for parents to impress that urgency on the child's heart.

"Knowing, therefore, the terror of the Lord, we persuade men" (2 Corinthians 5:11). "God . . . reconciled us to Himself through Jesus Christ, and has given us the ministry of reconciliation, that is, that God was in Christ reconciling the world to Himself, not imputing their trespasses to them, and has committed to us the word of reconciliation. Now then, we are ambassadors for Christ, as though God were pleading through us: we implore you on Christ's behalf, be reconciled to God" (vv. 18–20).

"Seek the LORD while He may be found, call upon Him while He is near. Let the wicked forsake his way, and the unrighteous man his thoughts; let him return to the LORD, and He will have mercy on him; and to our God, for He will abundantly pardon" (Isaiah 55:6–7).

TEACH YOUR CHILDREN *DILIGENTLY*

Some parents will look at an outline like that and feel grossly underqualified to teach so much, as well as deal with the inevitable questions children raise. Add the essential requirement (which we'll cover in future chapters) that the parent's character and conduct must be consistent with what we teach, and there's no doubt that fulfilling Deuteronomy 6:6–7 is a formidable task. Woe to the parent who approaches this task half-heartedly or whose follow-through is lackadaisical.

Look again at Deuteronomy 6:7, "You shall teach [these things] *diligently* to your children, and shall talk of them when you sit in your house, when you walk by the way, when you lie down, and when you rise up" (emphasis added). Diligence is absolutely essential to what God demands of parents.

That means if you think your own grasp of spiritual truth is insufficient to teach these things to your children, you had better start learning immediately. God holds you responsible as a *Christian*, and not merely as a *parent*, to have enough knowledge of elementary gospel truth so that you can teach others (Hebrews 5:12). One of your basic duties as a Christian is teaching and admonishing fellow believers (Colossians 3:16). Another essential duty is teaching unbelievers the truth of the gospel (Matthew 28:19–20). If your grasp of spiritual truth is such that you fear you are incapable of teaching even your own children, it may mean you have not been careful in fulfilling some of your most basic responsibilities as a Christian—unless you are a brand new believer yourself. But whether you are a babe in Christ or someone who has been indifferent, it is now your duty to begin studying to show yourself approved unto God, so that you can be obedient both as a parent and as a Christian. This requires much diligence.

Again, we emphasize that parenting is not as complex as many people imagine. But neither is it *easy.* The demands on parents are constant. There is no time to sit back and coast. The task of *teaching* that's required is a never-ending, full-time occupation. There is much to teach, and an endless supply of opportunities. Be sure you make the most of those opportunities.

Four

Teaching Your Children Wisdom

*A wise son makes a glad father, but a foolish son
is the grief of his mother.*

—PROVERBS 10:1

FOUR

❦

Teaching Your Children Wisdom

Teaching children the gospel by no means exhausts the parents' teaching responsibility. Also bound up in the principle of Deuteronomy 6:6–7 is the duty of teaching our children wisdom for life. The gospel is the necessary starting-point, because "the fear of the LORD is the *beginning* of wisdom" (Psalm 111:3). No one is truly wise who rejects or disregards the gospel message.

But beyond the basic truths of the gospel are also many vital biblical lessons about character, integrity, justice, prudence, discernment, and all the practical issues of life. Parents are charged with the duty of carefully training their children with godly wisdom in all such matters.

The Book of Proverbs in the Old Testament is an inspired summary of such practical wisdom. The sayings recorded there were assembled by Solomon for his son's sake. Most of them were actually written by Solomon, but some are others' proverbs, collected by Solomon. The best wisdom of several ancient sages is thus compiled in Solomon's Book of Proverbs with the seal of divine inspiration guaranteeing that these sayings are "profitable for doctrine, for reproof, for correction, for instruction in righteousness" (2 Timothy 3:16).

Proverbs is therefore a fitting textbook for parents, and fathers in particular, to teach their children the kind of practical wisdom necessary for prosperity in this life. It is an inspired book of wisdom from the wisest father who ever lived, a vital compendium of the sort of practical wisdom *all* parents need to pass on to their children.

Solomon includes an admonition to his own son in the opening verses: "My son, hear the instruction of your father, and do not forsake the law of your mother; for they will be a graceful ornament on your head, and chains about your neck" (Proverbs 1:8–9). Similar admonitions are repeated elsewhere in Proverbs: "My son . . . receive my words, and treasure my commands within you" (2:1); "My son, do not forget my law, but let your heart keep my commands" (3:1); "Hear, my children, the instruction of a father, and give attention to know understanding" (4:1); "Hear, my son, and receive my sayings, and the years of your life will be many" (4:10); "My son, give attention to my words; incline your ear to my sayings" (4:20); "My son, pay attention to my wisdom; lend your ear to my understanding" (5:1); "My son, keep your father's command, and do not forsake the law of your mother" (6:20); "My son, keep my words, and treasure my commands within you" (7:1); and many other verses throughout the book. These were Solomon's tender admonitions to his own son, urging him to pay careful heed to these lessons about life.

Such admonitions also apply to our children, and if we hope to teach well, we too must master the wisdom of Scripture and live consistently so that these principles of wisdom are reflected in our own character.

Solomon himself is an object lesson about the dangers of an inconsistent life. Solomon was, in intellectual terms, the wisest man who ever lived. First Kings 4:29 says of him, "God gave Solomon wisdom and exceedingly great understanding, and largeness of heart like the sand on the seashore. Thus Solomon's wisdom excelled the wisdom of all the men of the East and all the wisdom of Egypt. For he was wiser than all men." God Himself told Solomon, "I have given you a wise and understanding heart, so that there has not been anyone like you before you, nor shall any like you arise after you" (3:12).

So there was no deficiency whatsoever in the *content* of Solomon's instruction to his son. Yet by way of *example,* Solomon failed, and failed miserably. For example, Solomon included several warnings about the dangers of being seduced by the wrong kind of women (Proverbs 2:16–19; 5:3–13, 20; 6:23–29; 7:5–27; 22:14; 31:30). But Scripture says this about Solomon's own life: "King Solomon loved many foreign women, as well as the daughter of Pharaoh: women of the Moabites, Ammonites, Edomites, Sidonians, and Hittites from the nations of whom the LORD had said to the children of Israel, 'You shall not intermarry with them, nor they with you. Surely they will turn away your hearts after their gods.' Solomon clung to these in love" (1 Kings 11:1–2).

And partly because of Solomon's failure to live according to the wisdom God had given him, Solomon's son Rehoboam rejected his father's teaching (12:6–11).

It does no good to teach our children sound wisdom and then live a life that contradicts what we are teaching. In fact, there may be no surer way to provoke your children to despise and discard the wisdom of the Lord. The price of parental hypocrisy is unbearably high.

In Solomon's case, that sort of hypocrisy not only caused his son to fail, but it also tore apart the entire Israelite nation and led to an apostasy from which Israel never did recover. Scripture tells us this:

> The LORD became angry with Solomon, because his heart had turned from the LORD God of Israel, who had appeared to him twice, and had commanded him concerning this thing, that he should not go after other gods; but he did not keep what the LORD had commanded. Therefore the LORD said to Solomon, "Because you have done this, and have not kept My covenant and My statutes, which I have commanded you, I will surely tear the kingdom away from you and give it to your servant. Nevertheless I will not do it in your days, for the sake of your father David; I will tear it out of the hand of your son. However I will not tear away the whole kingdom; I will give one tribe to your son for the sake of my servant David, and for the sake of Jerusalem which I have chosen." (1 Kings 11:9–14)

Solomon's *instructions* to his son were sound. But the *example* he set nullified his wise counsel. His own life was inconsistent with his teaching. There is no greater mistake a parent can make.

AN INTRODUCTION TO THE WISDOM OF SOLOMON

A proverb is a wise principle stated in concise, and often poetic, terms. The pithy form has a purpose; it is a mnemonic device, making the wisdom of the proverb easy to retain.

As we noted in chapter one, the sayings in Proverbs should be regarded as *truisms,* not inviolable *promises.* For example, many verses in Proverbs suggest that calamity belongs to the wicked and prosperity to the righteous. Proverbs 11:8 says, "The righteous is delivered from trouble, and it comes to the wicked instead." That is generally true as a principle, but it is certainly not a rule without exceptions. We know that the wicked *do* sometimes prosper (Psalm 73:3; Jeremiah 12:1). And trouble *does* sometimes come to the righteous (2 Thessalonians 1:4–7). "There is a just man who perishes in his righteousness, and there is a wicked man who prolongs life in his wickedness" (Ecclesiastes 7:15). So the truism of Proverbs 11:8 isn't meant to be a promise that can be claimed in every specific situation.

It *is* generally true, however, that prosperity belongs to the righteous, and trouble comes to the wicked. Whatever prosperity the wicked enjoy and whatever suffering the righteous must endure are always temporary. So the wisdom the proverb conveys is certainly sound. Wicked behavior is utter folly, and righteousness is superior to wickedness, even from a *practical* standpoint. *That's* the lesson Solomon aimed to teach his son.

Notice how the depth of Solomon's wisdom contrasts sharply with most of the parenting advice being published today. Much of the modern material, including some labeled "Christian," is appallingly trivial by comparison to the wisdom Solomon sought to pass along to his son. Today's typical advice for fathers says, "Be a buddy to your son. Go places with him. Teach him about sports. Take him to a ball game. Have fun doing 'guy' things with him." Or, "Compliment your daughter. Notice how she dresses, and find something to praise. Show her affection. Have special nights on which you take her out. Be sensitive to her emotional ups and downs. Listen to her." And on it goes. Some of those things may be helpful on a certain level, but you can concentrate your energies on *all* those things and still fail to teach your children wisdom. If that happens, you will not succeed as a parent.

Furthermore, if you focus your energies on the trivial things, you'll raise shallow children who set their affections on trivial things. Devote your energies to teaching profound things, and you'll raise children of profound character who love wisdom. Real wisdom for life is the most valuable gift parents can pass on to their children—certainly superior to any material legacy. And what better place to turn to for wisdom to teach our children than an inspired book written for just that purpose?

Wisdom is the theme throughout the Book of Proverbs. The word *wisdom* dominates the book. Sometimes synonyms (or near synonyms) are used, such as *instruction, understanding,* or *discretion.* All those words are simply elements of real wisdom. To know, to understand, to be instructed, and to have discretion is to act wisely. Note carefully that true wisdom includes not simply intellectual content, but practical conduct as well. Wisdom encompasses not only what we *know* but also what we *do* and sometimes what we *don't do.* "A wise man fears and departs from evil" (14:16). "He who restrains his lips is wise" (10:19). "He who wins souls is wise" (11:30). "He who heeds counsel is wise" (12:15). Solomon repeatedly made the connection between wisdom and righteous conduct. It's unfortunate that he did not stay true to this principle in his own later life.

When all is said and done, what is *done* is as vital to true wisdom as what is *said.* In short, genuine biblical wisdom involves living righteously. And as parents, it is our duty not only to teach our sons and daughters the concepts of wise living, but also to model wisdom for them, so that they understand that this wisdom is the noblest and purest pursuit of all.

THE PERSONIFICATION OF WISDOM

In Proverbs 1:20–21 wisdom is personified: "Wisdom calls aloud outside; she raises her voice in the open squares. She cries out in the chief concourses, at the openings of the gates in the city she speaks her words." What is she crying out about? She is calling simple-minded people to turn away from being naïve. She is crying out for scoffers and fools to turn to wisdom (v. 22).

The whole Book of Proverbs echoes that call to wisdom. In chapter 2 verses 1–6, the voice of the father encourages his son to seek wisdom:

> My son, if you receive my words,
> And treasure my commands within you,
> So that you incline your ear to wisdom,
> And apply your heart to understanding;
> Yes, if you cry out for discernment,
> And lift up your voice for understanding,
> If you seek her as silver,
> And search for her as for hidden treasures;
> Then you will understand the fear of the Lord,
> And find the knowledge of God.
> For the LORD gives wisdom;
> From His mouth come knowledge and understanding.

The father's primary appeal to his son is this: "Pursue wisdom."

The whole of chapter eight is about pursuing wisdom. Verse eleven says, "Wisdom is better than rubies, and all the things one may desire cannot be compared with her." Then wisdom personified speaks again:

> I, wisdom, dwell with prudence,
> And find out knowledge and discretion.
> The fear of the LORD is to hate evil;
> Pride and arrogance and the evil way
> And the perverse mouth I hate.
> Counsel is mine, and sound wisdom;
> I am understanding, I have strength.

By me kings reign,

And rulers decree justice.

By me princes rule, and nobles,

All the judges of the earth.

I love those who love me,

And those who seek me diligently will find me.

Riches and honor are with me,

Enduring riches and righteousness.

My fruit is better than gold, yes, than fine gold,

And my revenue than choice silver.

I traverse the way of righteousness,

In the midst of the paths of justice,

That I may cause those who love me to inherit wealth,

That I may fill their treasuries. (Proverbs 8: 12–21)

The verses that follow have clear overtones that identify *Christ* as the true personification of all wisdom:

The LORD possessed me at the beginning of His way,

Before His works of old.

I have been established from everlasting,

From the beginning, before there was ever an earth.

When there were no depths I was brought forth,

When there were no fountains abounding with water.

Before the mountains were settled,

Before the hills, I was brought forth;

While as yet He had not made the earth or the fields,

Or the primeval dust of the world.

When He prepared the heavens, I was there,

When He drew a circle on the face of the deep,

When He established the clouds above,

When He strengthened the fountains of the deep,

When He assigned to the sea its limit,

So that the waters would not transgress His command,

When He marked out the foundations of the earth,

Then I was beside Him as a master craftsman;

And I was daily His delight,

Rejoicing always before Him. (Proverbs 8: 22–30)

Christ thus embodies and personifies all authentic wisdom. He *is* the sum of all wisdom. "In [Him] are hidden all the treasures of wisdom and knowledge" (Colossians 2:3). And so again we see that the parents' teaching task boils down to teaching our children about Christ. Whether we're teaching them the gospel, or teaching them wisdom for life in general, the proper focus of all our instruction is Christ.

VITAL LESSONS FOR LIFE

Obviously, it's not possible in a book of this scope to do a thorough study of all the wisdom in Proverbs. But I have selected ten principles from this book that are the kind of lessons parents should teach their children. These principles make a significant start, and parents can glean from them a methodology for studying and applying the Proverbs that will yield many more lessons in wisdom for your children.

If your children learn these lessons, they will be more able to be a blessing to you, and they will be blessed by God. Notice, too, as we go through these principles, how closely spiritual wisdom and practical wisdom are always intertwined.

Teach Your Children to Fear Their God

Proverbs 1:7 says, "The fear of the LORD is the beginning of knowledge." Proverbs 9:10 repeats the theme: "The fear of the LORD is the beginning of wisdom, and the knowledge of the Holy One is understanding." Again we see that all genuine wisdom starts with fearing God. The fear of God is the one true foundation of the wisdom we must teach our kids.

By now this is already a familiar point. We've visited it repeatedly throughout the opening chapters of this book. It was in a sense the whole theme of chapters two and three. It may begin to sound redundant, but Scripture itself repeatedly stresses this point. Parents who *miss* the point have no excuse. Successful parenting literally begins with instilling in your children a proper fear of God.

I mentioned briefly in chapter three that this is not a cowardly, craven fear. It's not a phobia. It's not the sort of fear that regards God as malevolent. There's no trace of abhorrence or enmity in true godly fear.

This fear has two aspects. The first is *reverence*. It is a sacred awe of God's utter holiness. It involves the kind of respect and veneration that results in fear in the presence of such absolute majesty.

The second aspect is *fear of God's displeasure*. Genuine faith acknowledges God's right to chasten, His right to punish, and His right to judge. Therefore, in the presence of God, true wisdom trembles with a holy, healthy sense of terror and apprehension. *Fear* is the right word for it. The deeper our sense of our own guilt, the more profound should be our dread of God's displeasure.

When you teach your children about God, be sure to give them a full appreciation of *all* His attributes. Children need to know, even from the earliest age, that God is angry with the wicked, and He *will* punish evildoers (Psalm 7:11–13). Material designed for young children too often presents only the gentle, meek, and mild attributes of God. He is portrayed as an always-benign grandfatherly being—an insipid, man-made god, more like Santa than the God of Scripture. This is a very serious mistake, and I believe it accounts for the careless attitude so many in our society have toward God. They mistakenly assume that whatever God's nature, He will ultimately be harmless and kindly, even toward those who have disobeyed Him. That is the impression many children take away from the typical Sunday school lesson. But it is not the God of Scripture. Take care not to teach your children such a wrong perspective of God.

There is a true sense in which you must teach your children to fear God, and especially to fear His displeasure. You have not satisfied the responsibilities of parenthood when you have made your child submit to you. If you are consistent and firm in your discipline, your child may obey you because he or she fears violating your standards. That is a fairly easy thing to achieve. But it is not the proper goal of biblical parenting. Your child should fear violating *God's* standard, not merely yours. You are only an intermediary with the responsibility of teaching your child to fear *God*. If your children grow up fearing only *your* displeasure but not God's, what will they do when you are not there?

Your children need to grow up with an awareness that when they do wrong, it doesn't just irritate Mommy; it doesn't just antagonize Daddy; it doesn't just cause disorder in the family. But when they disobey, they set themselves against a holy God who deals out consequences for those who violate His righteous principles.

My goal as a father was not merely to have my children fear being chastened by their father. I wanted them to fear being chastened by their God. I wanted them to fear *my* discipline, too, of course, but that was incidental. I knew I could not always be around to hold them accountable, but God is. And the consequences of violating His will are infinitely greater than any disobedience on the human level. Unfortunately, few kids today grow up with that awareness. Kids are no longer taught to fear God, and it shows, at every level of society.

From the very earliest age, teach your children that sin is a capital offense against a holy God. Teach them that God is not mocked, and they will reap the bitter consequences of whatever sin they sow. Instill in them a healthy fear of God. Without that sort of fear, genuine repentance is not even possible.

Furthermore, when your children fear God, they will also fear sin. That's certainly a healthy fear to cultivate. It will spare them much grief in life by keeping them from evil (16:6).

It may also literally prolong their lives. Proverbs 10:27 says, "The fear of the LORD prolongs days, but the years of the wicked will be shortened." Want to give your son or daughter a rich, full life? Teach them the fear of the Lord. "The fear of the LORD is a fountain of life, to turn one away from the snares of death" (14:27). "The fear of the LORD leads to life, and he who has it will abide in satisfaction; he will not be visited with evil" (19:23).

Fearing the Lord is more profitable than wealth. "Better is a little with the fear of the LORD, than great treasure with trouble" (15:16).

"In the fear of the LORD there is strong confidence, and His children will have a place of refuge" (14:26).

Teach Your Children to Guard Their Minds

Here's a principle parents must emphasize more than ever, especially in the age of the Internet: Teach your children to guard their *minds.* Proverbs 4:23 says, "Keep your heart with all diligence, for out of it spring the issues of life." Scripture speaks of "the heart" as the seat of both the emotions and the intellect. It is often used as a synonym for the mind. "As he *thinks* in his heart, so is he" (23:7, emphasis added).

Our children must learn to guard their minds diligently. Never in human history have the forces of evil waged a campaign to capture human minds on the scale we are seeing today. As parents, we are partly responsible for guarding our children's minds. The onslaught against righteous thinking comes from several fronts: television, radio, movies, music, the Internet, and nowadays even from school curriculum. So the parent's task is indeed a formidable one.

Parents can, and must, protect children from exposure to the most unsavory aspects of modern entertainment and media. Monitor what they see and hear. Do not simply turn them loose on the Internet. Don't hand them the television remote and leave the room. It is all right to allow them some choice about what they will watch and listen to, but do not let them make those choices totally unsupervised. You have a right and a responsibility to help steer them toward what edifies and away from all that does not. I always encourage parents to set high standards in this area, not permitting children to expose themselves indiscriminately to any movies, music, television, or other things that aim to promote evil thoughts or feed evil appetites. All such choices need to be made with parental guidance, and with the utmost caution. The psalmist wrote, "I will set nothing wicked before my eyes" (Psalm 101:3).

But as discussed in chapter two, total isolation is no answer. No amount of isolationism could keep your children's hearts free from defilement anyway, because as fallen creatures they carry sinful desires and a sinful imagination around inside them just as you do. And frankly, there is no good way to shelter your children completely from all the evil influences in a society like ours. These days even billboards on our public thoroughfares convey messages designed to stir the most base kinds of fleshly appetites.

Realize, too, that you cannot teach your children to guard their hearts and minds merely by trying to shield them from external evil influences. You must also train them to be wise and discerning. You must teach them how to cultivate wholesome thoughts. As the apostle Paul wrote to the Philippians, "Whatever things are true, whatever things are noble, whatever things are just, whatever things are pure, whatever things are lovely, whatever things are of good report, if there is any virtue and if there is anything praiseworthy; meditate on these things" (Philippians 4:8).

Out of our thoughts comes our conduct. That is what Jesus meant when He said, "What comes out of a man, that defiles a man. For from within, out of the heart of men, proceed evil thoughts, adulteries, fornications, murders, thefts, covetousness, wickedness, deceit, lewdness, an evil eye, blasphemy, pride, foolishness. All these evil things come from within and defile a man" (Mark 7:20–22).

Our true character is therefore defined by what we *think,* not how we appear to others, not what we say and, ultimately, not even how we behave. The truest test of character is the thought life. As a man thinks, so is he (Proverbs 23:7).

Parents therefore have the task of helping program their children's minds with truth, kindness, faithfulness, honesty, integrity, loyalty, love, and all the other virtues that ought to shape their thinking. All of that is part of teaching our children to guard their thoughts.

Teach Your Children to Obey Their Parents

The first direct appeal Solomon makes to his son in the Book of Proverbs is this: "My son, hear the instruction of your father, and do not forsake the law of your mother" (1:8). The same theme runs throughout the book. In chapter four, he writes this:

> Hear, my children, the instruction of a father,
> And give attention to know understanding;

> For I give you good doctrine:
> Do not forsake my law.
> When I was my father's son,
> Tender and the only one in the sight of my mother,
> He also taught me, and said to me:
> "Let your heart retain my words;
> Keep my commands, and live. (Proverbs 4:1–4)

Then he takes up the same theme a couple of chapters later:

> My son, keep your father's command,
> And do not forsake the law of your mother.
> Bind them continually upon your heart;
> Tie them around your neck.
> When you roam, they will lead you;
> When you sleep, they will keep you;
> And when you awake, they will speak with you.
> For the commandment is a lamp,
> And the law a light;
> Reproofs of instruction are the way of life. (Proverbs 6:20–23)

And here's a picturesque warning to the wayward child: "The eye that mocks his father, and scorns obedience to his mother, the ravens of the valley will pick it out, and the young eagles will eat it" (30:17).

Parents *must* teach their children obedience. This is one of the most basic and obvious responsibilities of parenthood. If we are going to raise a generation of faithful children to live righteous lives, they must begin by learning to obey their parents. And it is the parents' solemn responsibility to teach them this. I constantly marvel at how many parents seem practically clueless when it comes to this responsibility. This is by no means an optional aspect of parenting. As the apostle points out in Ephesians 6:2–3, the first of the Ten Commandments accompanied by a promise for those who obeyed it was the Fifth Commandment: "Honor your father and your mother, that your days may be long upon the land which the LORD your God is giving you" (Exodus 20:12). It is the parents' responsibility to train the child to obey from the time the child learns the sound of the parents' voice.

That involves discipline and, when necessary, chastening and correction. Parents who fail to correct their disobedient children are displaying a shameful lack of love. "He who spares his rod hates his son, but he who loves him disciplines him promptly" (13:24). Proverbs 3:11–12 says, "My son, do not despise the chastening of the LORD, nor detest His correction; for whom the LORD loves He corrects, just as a father the son in whom he delights." Parents who truly love their children will reprove them when they disobey.

In other words, proper chastening is not merely for retribution; it really is in the child's best interest. It should not be regarded as a payback but as an aid to growth, something that edifies and strengthens the child. Chastening helps conform their minds to wisdom. It removes foolishness from their hearts. It can help deliver them from the misery of sin's consequences up to and including hell.

These are frequent themes in the Book of Proverbs. "Foolishness is bound up in the heart of a child; the rod of correction will drive it far from him" (22:15). "Do not withhold correction from a child, for if you beat him with a rod, he will not die. You shall beat him with a rod, and deliver his soul from hell" (23:13–14).

Note carefully that those verses expressly make corporal punishment—the rod—an essential part of parental discipline. When Solomon spoke of the rod, he employed a Hebrew term for a branch or a stick. Rods were used by shepherds as walking sticks, as instruments of defense, as standards of measurement, as tools to guide the sheep, and as implements of reproof to control wayward lambs. Occasionally someone will note all those possible uses of the rod and suggest that when Solomon spoke of the rod, perhaps he was speaking only of giving positive guidance and shepherdlike nurturing care to children, rather than advocating the use of the rod as an instrument of corporal punishment. But that suggestion utterly ignores Solomon's plain words. In 23:13–14, for example, he speaks of *beating* the child with the rod. Corporal punishment is unquestionably what he has in mind, and it is equally clear that Solomon regarded corporal punishment as an indispensable aspect of wise parenting. In other words, using the rod as an instrument of punishment is not at odds with the idea of nurturing and shepherding our children—it is an essential aspect of it. Parents cannot omit this aspect and delude themselves into thinking they are being good shepherds to their children.

The language of "beating" the child evokes images of child abuse for some. But Solomon is not sanctioning physical abuse or brutality. He is not giving parents encouragement to batter their children. The word translated "beat" both times it appears in Proverbs 23:13–14 simply means "to smite," with no necessary connotations about the lightness or the severity of the blow being administered. The context makes clear, however, that the purpose of striking the child is to inflict pain, not injury. The pain inflicted is designed not to injure the child, but to make the consequence of disobedience unforgettable. If your spanking leaves bruises or welts that are still visible the following day, you are striking the child too hard. Short, stinging strokes to the backside (where the natural padding is most plentiful), will not injure the child, but should be painful enough to make the consequences of disobedience sufficiently distasteful and unforgettable.

Proverbs 13:24 makes very clear that discipline is always to be administered with, and tempered by, love. Parents who administer chastening out of sheer fury or exasperation rather than love will find no support for that sort of discipline anywhere in Scripture. But neither does Scripture sanction a superficial love that is always lenient, indulgent, and permissive.

The love that leads to proper discipline is a strong and robust love that demands obedience and punishes disobedience because that is what is best for the child. The parent should be grieved by the need to administer punishment and can therefore grieve along with the child over the consequences of sin. Physical punishment, when saturated with that kind of love, is a very strong corrective.

Chastening should also be firm and consistent. "Chasten thy son while there is hope, and let not thy soul spare for his crying" (19:18, KJV). Don't be erratic with your discipline, and don't be so soft-hearted that you become overly lenient. Correction must be steady and unwavering, or it will not be effective. If parents are inconsistent, children will begin to regard the discipline as arbitrary and capricious.

"The rod and rebuke give wisdom, but a child left to himself brings shame to his mother" (29:15). A disobedient child makes not only a spiritual disaster but an anti-social personality and, very often, a criminal adult.

By the way, I do not personally buy many modern clinical excuses for childhood rebellion. More and more parents of unruly children are being told that their kids have afflictions such as Attention Deficit Disorder (ADD), Attention Deficit/Hyperactivity Disorder (ADHD), Antisocial Personality Disorder (APD), Oppositional Defiant Disorder (ODD), Histrionic Personality Disorder (HPD), and Bipolar Disorder (manic depression). I know of no known organic or biological cause for any of those "disorders." Most such diagnoses seem to me to be little more than high-sounding clinical terms that have been applied to lazy, selfish, defiant, or otherwise sinful conduct.

Nonetheless, many doctors automatically prescribe drugs for treatment of such ailments. Ritalin is a psychostimulant, amphetamine-type drug now being taken by more than two million children in the United States alone for the purpose of suppressing misbehavior. Drugs have thus replaced discipline for millions of parents. The drugs take less time; they are painless; and they need to be administered only once or twice a day.

A huge market for such drugs has been manufactured from the myth that misbehavior patterns in children are always pathological, rather than (as Solomon would say) sinful foolishness in the heart of the child. As soon as the drugs wear off, the misbehavior returns. And what will these children do as adults, if drugs were the only thing that suppressed their sinful behavior in childhood? Our nation's prisons are already filling up with answers to that question.

It may well be true that some children are naturally more prone to have short attention spans or other weaknesses that make learning a greater struggle for them. Obviously, many natural abilities, such as intelligence and creative aptitude, are largely shaped by genetic factors. It is also quite likely that there are genetic reasons or unknown biological causes for certain learning disabilities.

Learning difficulties per se, however, are not a moral issue. Disobedience, cruelty to other children, and disrespect for adults are. To attach a clinical name to chronic misbehavior and use it as an excuse for sinful behavior is a serious mistake. Disobedience is sinful, regardless of what factors shape the child's natural aptitude.

In other words, there are few excuses for a rebellious child. Scripture indicates that parents can and should teach their kids to obey. While this is undoubtedly a harder task with some kids than with others, it is *never* the parents' prerogative to drug an unruly child in place of disciplining him, no matter how many modern doctors are willing to classify chronic misbehavior as some kind of medical pathology. No matter what the child's reasons for misconduct, rebellion and disobedience are ultimately a *moral* malady—*sin*—and Scripture itself lays the responsibility for correction at the parents' feet.

Teach Your Children to Select Their Companions

No principle in child-rearing may be more vital and yet more neglected than this one: Teach your children to select their companions wisely. Solomon wrote, "He who walks with wise men will be wise, but the companion of fools will be destroyed" (Proverbs 13:20).

Parents must take the offensive on this. If you do not help your children select, and help them *learn* to select for themselves, the right kind of companions, the wrong kind of companions will inevitably select them. The responsibility of teaching children how to choose their friends wisely is therefore a fundamental element of successful biblical parenting.

The apostle Paul wrote, "Do not be deceived: 'Evil company corrupts good habits'" (1 Corinthians 15:33). Your kids' personal moral standards, the language they use, and the activities they engage in, will probably not rise above the lowest common denominator of their companions' standards. Rarely does a child have the capability to elevate himself beyond the constituent group in which he functions.

And bad influences among their friends pose a deadly danger.

"A little leaven leavens the whole lump" (1 Corinthians 5:6). It is a fact of human nature that young people are more prone to follow a bad example than they are to set a good example, especially if it means going against their peers.

In Proverbs 1:10 Solomon says to his son, "My son, if sinners entice you, do not consent." He wanted to make sure his son was not susceptible to being recruited into bad company. He cautioned his son that evildoers will always try to seduce the naïve by making evil sound exciting and adventurous. But Solomon told his son,

> If they say, "Come with us,
> Let us lie in wait to shed blood;
> Let us lurk secretly for the innocent without cause;
> Let us swallow them alive like Sheol,
> And whole, like those who go down to the Pit;
> We shall find all kinds of precious possessions,
> We shall fill our houses with spoil;
> Cast in your lot among us,
> Let us all have one purse";
> My son, do not walk in the way with them,
> Keep your foot from their path;
> For their feet run to evil,
> And they make haste to shed blood.
> Surely, in vain the net is spread
> In the sight of any bird;
> But they lie in wait for their own blood,
> They lurk secretly for their own lives. (Proverbs 1:11–18)

Young people today are being lured into precisely those kinds of crimes, and at a younger age than ever. Gang violence, pre-teen delinquency, and growing drug and alcohol abuse in our elementary schools are all trends that are closely related to young people's tendency to choose the wrong kind of companions. The ultimate failure in most cases belongs to parents who are not circumspect with regard to the friendships they permit their children to make.

Every parent must take this duty seriously. Even if you don't live in the kind of neighborhood where gangs might recruit your children, you can be certain that eventually your kids will face tremendous peer pressure to conform to a standard of conduct that is ungodly and sinful. You must teach them to select their companions wisely, so that they will not be intimidated into the wrong kinds of alliances. Don't let your children surround themselves with the wrong kind of peer pressure. Instruct them how to choose companions who lift them up.

It's impossible to overstate how important this principle is for our children. Wisdom is more or less epitomized by the ability to avoid deleterious companions:

> When wisdom enters your heart,
> And knowledge is pleasant to your soul,
> Discretion will preserve you;
> Understanding will keep you,
> To deliver you from the way of evil,
> From the man who speaks perverse things,
> From those who leave the paths of uprightness
> To walk in the ways of darkness;
> Who rejoice in doing evil,
> And delight in the perversity of the wicked;
> Whose ways are crooked,
> And who are devious in their paths. (Proverbs 2:10–15)

Teach Your Children to Control Their Lusts

The apostle Paul wrote Timothy, "Flee . . . youthful lusts; but pursue righteousness, faith, love, peace with those who call on the Lord out of a pure heart" (2 Timothy 2:22). It's significant that the apostle speaks of *youthful* lusts. The wise parent will realize that all adolescents develop powerful passions that can lead them in to tragedy unless they learn to control their lusts.

This is one of the dominant themes in the first few chapters of Proverbs. Solomon obviously regarded it as a critical truth to convey to his son. And no wonder. Failure in this very realm lay behind Solomon's own failures.

We return to Proverbs 2, exactly where we left off in the previous point. Solomon was saying that true wisdom has the effect of delivering us from evil companions and from the subtleties of evildoers. He continues this way:

> To deliver you from the immoral woman,
> From the seductress who flatters with her words,
> Who forsakes the companion of her youth,
> And forgets the covenant of her God.
> For her house leads down to death,
> And her paths to the dead;
> None who go to her return,
> Nor do they regain the paths of life. (Proverbs 2:16–19)

In other words, Solomon is telling his son that fornication can literally be fatal. He says the same thing in 5:3–5: "The lips of an immoral woman drip honey, and her mouth is smoother than oil; but in the end she is bitter as wormwood, sharp as a two-edged sword. Her feet go down to death, her steps lay hold of hell."

Some commentators think this is a reference to venereal disease, or possibly the kind of divine chastisement that costs the sinner his life (cf. 1 Corinthians 11:30; 1 John 5:16). But it is more likely that this is a reference to the legal penalty for adultery set forth in

Deuteronomy 22:22: "If a man is found lying with a woman married to a husband, then both of them shall die; the man that lay with the woman, and the woman; so you shall put away the evil from Israel."

But even in a society where the death penalty does not apply in cases of adultery, fornication is a soul-destroying and life-destroying sin. Solomon makes this point in Proverbs 6:23–33:

> For the commandment is a lamp,
> And the law a light;
> Reproofs of instruction are the way of life,
> To keep you from the evil woman,
> From the flattering tongue of a seductress.
> Do not lust after her beauty in your heart,
> Nor let her allure you with her eyelids.
> For by means of a harlot
> A man is reduced to a crust of bread;
> And an adulteress will prey upon his precious life.
> Can a man take fire to his bosom,
> And his clothes not be burned?
> Can one walk on hot coals,
> And his feet not be seared?
> So is he who goes in to his neighbor's wife;
> Whoever touches her shall not be innocent.
> People do not despise a thief
> If he steals to satisfy himself when he is starving.
> Yet when he is found, he must restore sevenfold;
> He may have to give up all the substance of his house.
> Whoever commits adultery with a woman lacks
>   understanding;
> He who does so destroys his own soul.

Wounds and dishonor he will get,
And his reproach will not be wiped away.

Fornication often brings a lifelong reproach. Many lives have been utterly destroyed by a single act of adultery. The spouse of an adulterer may find it forever impossible to regain the trust that was broken. Even if the offense is forgiven and the marriage saved, a measure of distrust often lingers for life. The sin itself carries a stigma that may be impossible to escape. If you want to understand the gravity of this, remember that men are not qualified to serve as elders and deacons in the church unless they are "above reproach" (1 Timothy 3:2, 10, NASB). When an elder or deacon falls to an act of fornication, he acquires a reproach that may attach itself to him for the rest of his life. And that means permanent disqualification. It is a heavy price to pay, but such is the reproach associated with this kind of sin.

Proverbs 7 takes up the theme again. And here Solomon wants to underscore in a graphic way the dangers of naiveté and the importance of not giving in to unbridled lust. Almost the entire chapter is devoted to a scenario featuring a seductress and her naive victim, "A young man devoid of understanding" (v. 7). This reckless, irresponsible, feather-headed dolt deliberately wanders into temptation. He is in a part of town where he should not be. The scenario is set as if Solomon is at the window looking out through the lattice, describing what he sees:

For at the window of my house
I looked through my lattice,
And saw among the simple,
I perceived among the youths,
A young man devoid of understanding,
Passing along the street near her corner;

And he took the path to her house
In the twilight, in the evening,
In the black and dark night. (Proverbs 7: 6–9)

Here's the victim. He is a victim not only of the seductress but also of his own sinful naiveté and his own evil desires. He knows full well where he is going. He's deliberately taking the path to an immoral woman's house, passing the street near her corner. He may not have any particular evil plans beyond walking by her house to see what will happen, but he is in a neighborhood where he ought not be, willfully exposing himself to temptation. That kind of behavior is the genesis of nearly every sin of immorality. If we teach our children not to walk where it is slippery, we minimize the opportunities for them to fall.

But here is a fellow wandering in the twilight on the wrong side of town, and he becomes prey to the wiles of a harlot:

And there a woman met him,
With the attire of a harlot, and a crafty heart.
She was loud and rebellious,
Her feet would not stay at home.
At times she was outside, at times in the open square,
Lurking at every corner.
So she caught him and kissed him;
With an impudent face she said to him:
"I have peace offerings with me;
Today I have paid my vows
So I came out to meet you,
Diligently to seek your face,
And I have found you." (Proverbs 7:10–15)

That is what is known as the direct approach to seduction. She seizes him, kisses him, and boldly propositions him. She tells him she has been under a temporary religious vow of celibacy, but now the vow is over. This is undoubtedly a lie, but it is her way of inviting him to celebrate the end of her celibacy. This is a direct solicitation to an act of fornication.

She tells him, "I came out to meet you," as if he is just the one she was looking for. That is another lie, of course, because she would have propositioned any man who crossed her path.

She makes her immoral intentions unmistakable:

> I have spread my bed with tapestry,
> Colored coverings of Egyptian linen.
> I have perfumed my bed
> With myrrh, aloes, and cinnamon.
> Come, let us take our fill of love until morning;
> Let us delight ourselves with love.
> For my husband is not at home;
> He has gone on a long journey;
> He has taken a bag of money with him,
> And will come home on the appointed day. (Proverbs 7:16–20)

She is enticing him by appealing to every kind of lust. The fine tapestry, the perfume, and the spices are all sensual attractions, erotic lures for the naïve victim. She promises him he will be safe, because her husband is far away on business, with lots of money to spend, not scheduled to return for a long time. Thus she erases both his scruples and all his fears with her cunning seduction.

But hidden behind her flattering words and temptress charms lies a deadly danger. Her real design is to kill him, probably to steal whatever money or valuables he is carrying. Like all prostitutes, she has no interest in romance; she only wants his wallet and his wealth—and she is willing to do anything to get it:

> With her enticing speech she caused him to yield,
> With her flattering lips she seduced him.
> Immediately he went after her, as an ox goes to the slaughter,
> Or as a fool to the correction of the stocks,
> Till an arrow struck his liver.
> As a bird hastens to the snare,
> He did not know it would cost his life. (Proverbs 7: 21–23)

The moral to Solomon's tale is a truth all parents need to teach their children about the deadly dangers of succumbing to fleshly lusts:

> Now therefore, listen to me, my children;
> Pay attention to the words of my mouth:
> Do not let your heart turn aside to her ways,
> Do not stray into her paths;
> For she has cast down many wounded,
> And all who were slain by her were strong men.
> Her house is the way to hell,
> Descending to the chambers of death. (Proverbs 7:24–27)

Teach Your Children to Enjoy Their Spouses

There's a flip side to the prior lesson. Teach them to channel their youthful passions toward righteous ends. Specifically, teach them to reserve their sexual passions for their spouses alone, and then teach them to be faithful in marriage.

Proverbs 5:15 says, "Drink water from your own cistern, and running water from your own well." That's a metaphor. Solomon was telling his son he should be faithful to his own wife, and not seek gratification for his sexual desires outside the bounds of his marriage. That verse follows immediately after one of Solomon's warnings about the dangers of the harlot, and it is further explained by verses 18–20:

> Let your fountain be blessed,
> And rejoice with the wife of your youth.
> As a loving deer and a graceful doe,
> Let her breasts satisfy you at all times;
> And always be enraptured with her love.
> For why should you, my son, be enraptured by an immoral woman,
> And be embraced in the arms of a seductress?

Teach your children that the only righteous place to find gratification of their sexual desires is from their own spouses. Solomon wrote an entire book of the Bible—Song of Solomon—celebrating the joys of the marital relationship. Unfortunately, Solomon himself took multiple wives, destroying the perfect union between one man and one woman that marriage was supposed to be (Genesis 2:24). Nonetheless, Song of Solomon stands as an inspired song about what the ideal marriage relationship is supposed to be.

First Thessalonians 4:3–5 says, "For this is the will of God, your sanctification: that you should abstain from sexual immorality; that each of you should know how to possess his own vessel in sanctification and honor." "Vessel" in that verse could be a reference to the wife, the weaker vessel (1 Peter 3:7), or it could be a reference to the person's own body. Either way, it enjoins faithfulness within the bonds of marriage, which in God's design is a union between *two* people who become *one* flesh (Ephesians 5:31).

Parents, don't make the mistake Solomon did. Teach this lesson to your children by example as well as by precept. Show them by the way you treat your spouse and by the things you say to one another that true contentment and full satisfaction are found only within the covenant of marriage.

Teach Your Children to Watch Their Words

In Proverbs 4:24, Solomon tells his son, "Put away from you a deceitful mouth, and put perverse lips far from you." Parents need to teach their children to watch their words. Speak truth. Say what edifies, not what injures others. And keep your words pure.

I can testify that as a child growing up this was one of the lessons my parents worked hardest to teach me. Therefore, as an adult, I never even think of using obscene words. I am probably as unlikely as any grownup on earth to use cursing or profanity. No doubt that is because as a child I had my mouth washed out with soap numerous times for words I couldn't even understand or pronounce correctly. To this day, when I overhear someone else using vile language, I start to taste the soap!

Solomon's proverbs are full of reminders about the importance of watching one's words: "The mouth of the righteous is a well of life" (10:11). "The tongue of the righteous is choice silver" (v. 20). "The lips of the righteous feed many" (v. 21). "The lips of the righteous know what is acceptable" (v. 32). "There is one who speaks rashly like the thrusts of a sword, but the tongue of the wise brings healing" (12:18, NASB). "The lips of the wise disperse knowledge" (15:7). "The heart of the wise teaches his mouth, and adds learning to his lips" (16:23). "The lips of knowledge are a precious jewel" (20:15).

And take special notice of Proverbs 12:22: "Lying lips are an abomination to the LORD, but those who deal truthfully are His delight." One lesson we always especially reinforced with our children was the importance of telling the truth. The pain attached to the consequences of lying was always double the pain of any other offense. Of course, none of them wanted to be caught in an act of disobedience. But if they disobeyed and lied about it, the consequences were worse by magnitudes. And so we taught them always to speak the truth. This is a vital lesson, because if a person can train his conscience to live with a lie, that person will be susceptible to *any* sin. If you can cover your sin with a lie, and if you condition your conscience to tolerate the lie, your conscience will in effect become useless to keep you from *any* sin.

Here's another important lesson about watching your words: "In the multitude of words sin is not lacking, but he who restrains his lips is wise" (10:19). Teach your children that it is often wiser *not* to talk. James wrote, "No man can tame the tongue. It is an unruly evil, full of deadly poison" (James 3:8). The mouths of fools are filled with strife, ruin, slander, belittlement, gossip, disgrace, lies, mischief, perversity. So teach your children that it is often best not to speak at all.

Teach Your Children to Pursue Their Work

While you're at it, teach them the value of hard work: "Go to the ant, you sluggard! Consider her ways and be wise, which, having no captain, overseer or ruler, provides her supplies in the summer, and gathers her food in the harvest" (Proverbs 6:6–8).

Almost anyone will work hard, or *appear* to work hard, when the boss is watching. But the ant works hard even though it has no overseer. Your children will work if you stand there with a whip.

But will they work if you don't? They're going to have to learn to work on their own initiative if they are going to be successful in life.

They also need to be taught how to plan ahead. The ant knows to prepare her food in the summer, anticipating the coming winter. Do your children know how to plan and work for their future needs? This is another vital lesson wise parents must teach their children.

Otherwise our kids will grow up to be sluggards.

> How long will you slumber, O sluggard?
> When will you rise from your sleep?
> A little sleep, a little slumber,
> A little folding of the hands to sleep;
> So shall your poverty come on you like a prowler,
> And your need like an armed man. (Proverbs 6: 9–11)

A sluggard is a lazy person. Or we might say that the sluggard is an otherwise ordinary person with too many excuses, too many refusals, and too many postponements. He procrastinates. He stalls. He does what he enjoys and delays what he finds unpleasant. But he will suffer hunger, poverty, and failure. He forfeits tomorrow's harvest for the sake of today's leisure. He wants but he won't work. The seed of his failure is his own slothfulness. It is one of the worst possible character flaws. Parents must not permit their children to develop habits of idleness and sloth.

On the other hand, the person who pursues his work earns a good living, has plenty of food, and earns respect. "Do you see a man who excels in his work? He will stand before kings; he will not stand before unknown men" (22:29). "He who has a slack hand becomes poor, but the hand of the diligent makes rich. He who gathers in summer is a wise son; he who sleeps in harvest is a son who causes shame" (10:4–5). Teach your kids those lessons.

Teach Your Children to Manage Their Money

Once your children are working, there's a ninth lesson they need to learn: how to manage their money wisely. Proverbs 3:9–10 says, "Honor the LORD with your possessions, and with the firstfruits of all your increase; so your barns will be filled with plenty, and your vats will overflow with new wine."

In other words, if you are generous with God, He will be generous with you. So honor the Lord with your money. That is the first rule of wise financial management. The firstfruits belong to the Lord. And not only the firstfruits, but *all* our possessions are to be used to the glory of God. Therefore, if you want your sons and daughters to know the fullness of God's blessing, teach them how to give generously to God, and teach them how to use their resources to honor Him.

That tops the list of positive lessons about money—we should use it to honor the Lord. There are many other positive lessons.

Generosity is a wiser financial policy than miserliness (11:24–26). Kindness to the poor unleashes the Lord's blessings (19:17; 22:9). And (as discussed above) the wise person works hard and plans for the future (10:4–5).

There are negative lessons, too. Proverbs 15:27, for example, teaches the folly of seeking financial gain through evil means: "He who is greedy for gain troubles his own house, but he who hates bribes will live." Proverbs 6:1–5 describes the dangers of co-signing with either friends or strangers in get-rich-quick schemes.

There are still more: "Do not overwork to be rich" (23:4). "He who trusts in his riches will fall" (11:28). "He who oppresses the poor to increase his riches, and he who gives to the rich, will surely come to poverty" (22:16).

Notice how Scripture repeatedly links moral truth and financial principles. How one manages one's money is a moral and spiritual issue. Make sure your children understand this.

Teach Your Children to Love Their Neighbors

Finally, teach your kids to love their neighbors. Teach them to value kindness and mercy and compassion:

> Do not withhold good from those to whom it is due,
> When it is in the power of your hand to do so.
> Do not say to your neighbor, "Go, and come back,
> And tomorrow I will give it,"
> When you have it with you.
> Do not devise evil against your neighbor,
> For he dwells by you for safety's sake. (Proverbs 3:27–29)

The command to love one's neighbor was a fundamental tenet of Moses' law: "You shall love your neighbor as yourself: I am the LORD" (Leviticus 19:18).

In Jesus' day, certain rabbis had diluted this law by saying it applies to *neighbors,* but not to *enemies.* Their version of the principle was, "You shall love your neighbor and hate your enemy" (Matthew 5:43). But Jesus pointed out that the commandment applies to enemies as well, for even God is merciful to the wicked (Matthew 5:44–48). Did you realize that the principle of loving one's enemies is also part of the wisdom recorded in Proverbs? Proverbs 25:21–22: "If your enemy is hungry, give him bread to eat; and if he is thirsty, give him water to drink; for so you will heap coals of fire on his head, and the Lord will reward you." The "coals of fire" heaped on his head refer to the burning of his own conscience. If you are kind to an enemy, and the fire in his own conscience melts him into kindness toward you, you will have made a friend of an enemy. You should teach your children, both by precept and by example, to treat their enemies that way. For our enemies are our neighbors, too. And Scripture clearly commands us to love them.

Jesus said the command to love one's neighbor is the second greatest commandment in all the law (Matthew 22:39). The greatest commandment, of course, is Deuteronomy 6:5: "You shall love the Lord your God with all your heart, with all your soul, and with all your strength." All the Law and the Prophets hang on those two commandments.

Notice that those same two principles are the first and the last of the ten I have listed here: Fear God, and love your neighbor. Everything in between fleshes out and amplifies those principles. Teach those principles to your kids, and you will raise your children to be wise.

That is the parents' duty. Parents, if you fail to teach your children to fear God, the devil will teach them to hate God. If you fail to teach them to guard their minds, the devil will teach them to have a corrupt mind. If you fail to teach them to obey their parents, the devil will teach them to rebel and break their parents' hearts. If you fail to teach them to select carefully their companions, the devil will choose companions for them. If you fail to teach them to control their lusts, the devil will teach them how to fulfill their lusts. If you fail to teach them to enjoy their own spouses, the devil will teach them to destroy their marriages. If you fail to teach them to watch their words, the devil will fill their mouths with filth. If you fail to teach them to pursue their work, the devil will make their laziness a tool of hell. If you fail to teach them to manage their money, the devil will teach them to squander it on riotous living. And if you fail to teach them to love their neighbors, the devil will teach them to love only themselves. We have a great responsibility to this generation and the next.

FIVE

The First Commandment with a Promise

Children, obey your parents in the Lord, for this is right. Honor your father and mother, so that it may be well with you, and that you may live long on the earth.

—EPHESIANS 6:1–3

FIVE

The First Commandment with a Promise

I n the previous chapter we briefly looked at the importance of teaching our children to obey their parents. In fact, that was one of ten essential principles of wisdom we examined from the Book of Proverbs. But teaching our children to obey their parents is more than a matter of merely pragmatic wisdom. It is also a bedrock moral principle, given a place of prominence among the Ten Commandments, and then emphasized repeatedly throughout Scripture. The child's duty to obey, and the parents' duty to teach obedience, certainly deserve our most thorough study and attention. Therefore in this chapter we return to delve even more deeply into this vital topic.

The Ten Commandments (Exodus 20:3–17) include two kinds of laws: *duties toward God* (have no other gods before Jehovah; make no graven images; don't take the Lord's name in vain; and keep the Sabbath holy); and *duties toward our neighbors* (honor your father and mother; don't kill; don't commit adultery; don't steal; don't bear false witness; and don't covet.) The four laws governing duties toward God are sometimes called the First Table of the law; the six laws governing conduct toward other people are known as the Second Table. The two tables are summed up in the first and second great commandments (Matthew 22:37–39): "You shall love the Lord your God with all your heart, and with all your soul, and with all your mind" (reiterating the theme of the First Table); and "You shall love your neighbor as yourself" (summarizing the duties of the Second Table).

The commandment about honoring father and mother takes first place in the Second Table of the law. In every child's life, this is the first important moral principle to be learned regarding behavior toward others. It is an indispensable and inviolable tenet of God's moral law, laying the foundation for every other principle about how we should treat our fellow human beings. And its importance is underscored not only by its position at the head of the Second Table, but also by the promise that accompanied the giving of the Fifth Commandment in Exodus 20:12: "Honor your father and your mother, *that your days may be prolonged in the land which the* LORD *your God gives you*" (emphasis added). The apostle Paul points out in Ephesians 6:2 that this is "the first commandment with a promise." As a matter of fact, it is the *only* commandment in the Decalogue that includes a promise. Of all the Ten Commandments, this one alone conveys a specific pledge of blessing and prosperity to those who obey it. According to the apostle, that fact is significant. It highlights the paramount importance of this commandment.

Scripture repeatedly underscores and expands the Fifth Commandment principle, teaching us that honoring our parents involves obeying them (Deuteronomy 21:18–21; Ephesians 6:1); honoring them with our words (Exodus 21:17; Leviticus 20:9; Proverbs 20:20; 30:11); showing them respect in every way

(Leviticus 19:3), even with our facial expressions'(Proverbs 30:17); hearkening to their counsel (Proverbs 23:22–25); and not treating them lightly in any sense (Deuteronomy 27:16; Ezekiel 22:7). A child's duty to honor parents does not cease even when the child becomes an adult. The inviolability of this law was affirmed by Jesus Himself, who condemned the Pharisees for inventing a way for grownups to circumvent the Fifth Commandment: "You are experts at setting aside the commandment of God in order to keep your tradition. For Moses said, 'Honor your father and your mother'; and, 'He who speaks evil of father or mother, is to be put to death'; but you say, 'If a man says to his father or his mother, whatever I have that would help you is Corban (that is to say, given to God),' you no longer permit him to do anything for his father or his mother; thus invalidating the word of God by your tradition which you have handed down; and you do many things such as that" (Mark 7:9–13).

They had taken an absolute and essential principle of righteousness and treated it as if it were a wax figure to be shaped any way they wanted. Christ rebuked them for allowing their own manmade doctrines and commandments to supersede God's own moral standard.

Some people like to debate about whether and to what degree the Ten Commandments are applicable in the Christian era. But the applicability of the Fifth Commandment is beyond dispute, because the apostle Paul affirmed and reiterated that commandment verbatim from Exodus 20:12 in Ephesians 6:1–3: "Children, obey your parents in the Lord, for this is right. Honor your father and mother (which is the first commandment with a promise), so that it may be well with you, and that you may live long on the earth" (NASB).

In the apostle's great summary of the duties of family life, that is the one obligation he expressly lays out for children. In fact, that is the only commandment in all of Scripture expressly addressed to children. All the child's *other* duties, including the responsibility of loving God and loving their brothers and sisters, are swept up into this one commandment: "Obey your parents." If the parents do *their* duty of bringing up their children "in the discipline and instruction of the Lord" (v. 4), the child who concentrates on obeying Mom and Dad will, through that obedience, learn to obey all the rest of God's principles. That is how Christian families are supposed to function.

In other words, the parent's first duty is to teach their children to obey them and then transfer that same obedience to God.

Now admittedly, teaching children to obey their parents is not always easy. At least it was not easy with my children. And it's not proving to be so with my grandchildren. It requires diligent effort on the parents' part.

Why? Here are three major reasons: The *corruption* all around our kids tends to defile them; the *curse* inside them tends to steer them the wrong way; and their own *childishness* makes them susceptible to many dangers.

TEACHING OBEDIENCE
IN A REBELLIOUS AGE

The world in which we live makes it especially difficult for us to teach our children obedience. There is *corruption all around them.* Our whole society is hostile to biblical truth, and this animosity toward God and the things of God shapes the culture in which we must raise our children. Sometime ago I clipped this letter from a young teenager to the editor of a national weekly news magazine. The young person wrote,

The economy is shot. The family unit is in trouble. Respect for authority is a joke. For the right price you can buy yourself a senator or a judge, or he is out buying himself a sixteen-year-old to use for a couple of hours. Money is worthless, and you're worthless without it. Stop worrying about *why* your son needs a drink before he can face his morning classes, or *why* your daughter went out and got pregnant. Just help them cope with the reality of life. Before throwing us into categories, just remember that we have to run this joint in thirty years when you die off or retire or starve on your Social Security. I leave it up to you: Either give us a little help and understanding, or put the world out of its misery and send up the missiles, and hope Mother Nature has better luck with the next thing that crawls up out of the slime.

How sad that someone's little baby developed such a cynical perspective on life so soon! But it does reflect something of the fear and distrust and disorientation and lostness of a whole generation of children and young people.

Secular society seems bent on teaching children to rebel against authority. Today's kids watch an average of thirty hours of television per week. Before she graduates from high school, the typical American teenager will have watched twenty thousand hours of television. The great majority of the programs she watches will portray authority figures as evil and rebellion as a virtue. She'll see all kinds of sin glamorized. Homosexuality will be presented as a normal, even noble, lifestyle choice. Murder, immorality, and drug use will be an essential part of the daily fare, so that even the grossest misdeeds will no longer even seem shocking. Thus inured to the exceeding sinfulness of sin, and inclined to distrust authority while romanticizing rebellion, she is poised to enter adulthood with very different moral values and a radically different worldview, from anyone in her great-grandparents' generation.

Is it any wonder that ten million children now have venereal disease, with five thousand more contracting sexually transmitted diseases every day? Is it any surprise that one in five teenagers uses drugs regularly? Are we really shocked that nearly a million young women now on the streets in America began working as prostitutes before age sixteen? Between seven and fourteen million children under the legal drinking age are already alcoholics. Millions of children seek help each year in psychiatric clinics. Satan-worship cults, school shootings, and teenagers who kill or abandon unwanted babies have all become virtually commonplace.

All these trends are the fruit of a society that sanctions and glorifies rebellion.

Scripture predicted that such a time would come: "But know this, that in the last days perilous times will come: For men will be lovers of themselves, lovers of money, boasters, proud, blasphemers, *disobedient to parents,* unthankful, unholy, unloving, unforgiving, slanderers, without self-control, brutal, despisers of good, traitors, headstrong, haughty, lovers of pleasure rather than lovers of God, having a form of godliness but denying its power. And from such people turn away" (2 Timothy 3:1–5, emphasis added)!

Notice that one of the characteristics of the last days is a widespread defiance toward parents, along with attitudes that are "unthankful, unholy, unloving." In the King James Version "unloving" is translated "without natural affection." The natural affection kids should have for their parents is systematically being destroyed by society's deliberate attack on parental authority.

Witness, for example, the policy now in effect in many public schools, enabling school nurses to pass out condoms and arrange abortions for children, yet denying the parents' right even to know when these things occur. Is it any wonder that kids in this society are increasingly rebellious, undisciplined, selfish, angry, bitter, frustrated, and destructive?

That is the kind of moral chaos in which today's children are growing up. The corruption of sin is all around them. Yet in the midst of all those influences, Christian parents are charged with the task of teaching their children to obey and respect authority, starting in the home.

CONFRONTING THE CHILD'S NATURAL BENT

In addition to the corruption on the outside, our kids must contend with *the curse of sin on the inside.* Not only is the world pressuring them to conform to ungodliness, but their own depravity causes them to be naturally prone to rebellion anyway. Both influences work constantly against parents who want to teach their children to obey. The parent who wants to raise an obedient child in today's world certainly cannot afford to approach the task half-heartedly.

What's more, the task of teaching our children to obey is not an assignment that can be completed in the early years of their childhood. These are lessons parents must continue to press until the time when the children become adults, leave father and mother, and cleave to their own spouses.

The Greek word translated "children" in Ephesians 6:1 is *teknon.* It is a broad term that applies to adult offspring as well as young toddlers. We know from elsewhere in Scripture, of course, that God's design for children is that they grow up, leave their parents, and be joined to spouses (Genesis 2:24). Obviously, when a child leaves the home, the parents are no longer the child's custodians, and the child's accountability decreases. Even after the child has left the home, however, the duty to respect and honor parents continues (Matthew 15:3–6). This respect for parents will come naturally to our children if they have learned obedience. They will retain throughout life a sensitivity and respect for their parents' views, even after they are no longer directly under their parents' authority.

But for children still under their parents' oversight, this verse calls for *obedience*. As long as they are under their parents' care—as long as parents are accepting the responsibility to provide for them—children must obey. They are under their parents' authority. This applies to children in their late teens no less than it applies to toddlers. Conversely, parents of teenagers have the same duty as parents of young children to be diligent in teaching them to obey. One of the worst things parents can do in the teenage years is give up and allow the child to rebel.

You must *teach* your children to obey. They are not naturally obedient. And if you think teaching them to obey will be a simple task, you are in for an unpleasant surprise. Your kids will be good at disobedience; you won't have to teach them that. No one ever had to explain to a child how to disobey. No parents have ever said to a toddler, "Let's do a little role playing so I can show you how to disobey." They have disobedience down very well; it comes naturally to them. They are experts in it from the very beginning. But obedience is something they must *learn.*

There is something in human nature that resists obedience. Tell the youngest toddler not to touch something on the coffee table, and he will go for that very item as soon as the parent's back is turned, if not sooner. Even the apostle Paul wrote about the human bias toward disobedience, noting that he was not exempt from it himself: "I would not have known about coveting if the Law had not said, 'You shall not covet.' But sin, taking opportunity through the commandment, produced in me coveting of every kind" (Romans 7:7–8). Kids are born knowing how to disobey. They must be *taught* to obey.

COMPENSATING FOR THE CHILD'S IMMATURITY

There's a great hue and cry today about liberating children. Social liberals are constantly talking about "children's rights." I even saw some literature from an ostensibly Christian organization urging parents to safeguard their children's rights, allowing them freedom of expression, privacy rights, the right to self-respect, and so on. According to this group, the biggest problem with kids today is that their parents are trampling their rights.

That's an echo of humanism; it is *not* a biblical perspective. When Scripture discusses the role of children in the family, the stress is on *responsibilities,* not *rights.* And every child's *main* responsibility is to obey his or her parents.

They have a basic problem, and it is that they are children. Even apart from their *sinful* tendencies, they are beset with human weaknesses—ignorance, immaturity, and frailties of all types—that make it necessary for them to obey the God-given higher authority of their parents. They are not ready for independence yet.

Even Jesus, sinless and perfect though He was, had to *learn* obedience as a human child. He never *dis*obeyed or acted sinfully, of course. In his humanness, He was all that a child could be. He was spotless, sinless, utterly untainted by the depravity that besets the rest of us. Yet as one "born under the law" (Galatians 4:4), He had to be subordinate to His earthly parents in accord with the Fifth Commandment. And He *did* submit to them (Luke 2:51).

This is a remarkable truth: Even Jesus *learned* obedience. In His humanity, obedience was something He had to be taught. Scripture says, "He learned obedience by the things which He suffered" (Hebrews 5:8). How can One who is sinlessly perfect, omniscient God in the flesh, *learn* anything, especially obedience? There's no way anyone can unpack all the mystery in that concept.

Nonetheless, Scripture is clear that Jesus *did* grow and learn, and His growth and learning as a child were like that of every other child, except for His sinlessness. He grew in four ways: "Jesus increased in wisdom and stature, and in favor with God and men" (Luke 2:52). He grew intellectually, physically, socially, and spiritually.

All children need to grow in those same four ways. As children, they are lacking in wisdom, they are wanting in physical stature, they need to grow in favor with God, and they have yet to acquire all the social skills they need to deal with other people. They are saddled with all the disadvantages of immaturity, plus the curse of sin, and it is our task to prepare them to face the corruption of the world.

HELPING THEM GROW IN WISDOM, IN STATURE, AND IN FAVOR WITH GOD AND MEN

How can we address our children's intellectual, physical, social, and spiritual needs? First it is helpful to have a good grasp of how profound those needs really are. Our kids are born ignorant, physically weak, spiritually deficient, and socially handicapped. Virtually everything they need to know about life must be taught to them.

The Intellectual Need

First, children have no discretion. They don't know what's good for them and what is not. Babies don't even know what's good to eat.

They'll put dirt, insects, or *anything* into their mouths. As they get a little older, they may show more taste than that, but even most teenagers, left to themselves, will choose things like sugared breakfast cereals and snack food, rather than vegetables and healthy foods.

Our kids must be taught discretion. In chapter four we listed ten principles of practical wisdom for life. Again, you must *teach* your kids those things. They will probably not discover them on their own. They are not born with such knowledge. They need to grow in wisdom.

And in the meantime, they must obey their parents, to make sure that their own deficiency in wisdom does not lead them astray.

The Physical Need

Second, children are born weak and unable to fend for themselves. Of all the higher mammals in God's creation, man alone is born with no ability whatsoever to sustain himself. Newborns are utterly unable to walk, crawl, or even roll over. Parents assume the responsibility of feeding them, changing them, making sure they get proper rest, and protecting them from all harm. If someone does *not* do all that for them, they will die.

And as they grow they gain strength, coordination, and the ability to move around on their own. Bit by bit they will gain a capacity for caring for themselves. Meanwhile, the parents' authority over them is part of the umbrella of protection God has given them, partly to compensate for their own physical weaknesses.

The Social Need

Third, children face a great need to learn some basic social graces. Children are not socially acclimated when they are born. In fact, children are totally self-centered. Their *only* concerns have to do with their own needs. They cry when they are hungry; they cry when they are tired; and they cry when they need to be changed. No infant ever cries because of his neighbor's needs. They feel no one else's pain. They scream only for their own. They have no sympathy. They have no interest in anything going on in the family. They are not attentive to the conversation. They make no effort to assist in anything. They just are preoccupied with themselves.

And as they grow, they need to be weaned from that self-centered worldview. But no child finds that easy. They don't want to share their toys. They want everything *right now.* They bicker with siblings and neighbors. They are still the center of their own world, and if they are going to mature enough to lose that perspective, they must be taught to do so.

Meanwhile, they must learn to obey, because their obedience to their parents is the very first step toward moving away from that immature, childish self-centeredness.

The Spiritual Need

Finally, children have an enormous spiritual need. They will not learn to love God naturally. They need to be taught spiritual truth, or they will never grow spiritually at all. Their spiritual ignorance, added to their natural depravity, works against them constantly.

The truth of Romans 8:7–8 applies to even the youngest unregenerate child: "Because the carnal mind is enmity against God; for it is not subject to the law of God, nor indeed can be. So then, those who are in the flesh cannot please God." They have a constitutional inability to obey God, to love Him, or to please Him. Their hearts are inclined toward evil. "Foolishness is bound up in the heart of a child" (Proverbs 22:15).

And with so many spiritual disadvantages working against children, God has set them under their parents' authority as a safeguard to help keep them from going astray spiritually.

Parental authority is therefore like a hothouse environment in which a child can grow more safely. If parents do not provide that protection through their authority over the child, all growth—intellectual, social, physical, and spiritual—will be stunted.

UNDERSTANDING OBEDIENCE

The term "obey" in Ephesians 6:1 is a simple, graphic term. The apostle Paul employs the Greek word *hupakouō*. The root from which that word is formed means "to hear," or "to heed," and it involves the idea of listening intently and conforming to a command. It implies an inward attitude of respect and honor, as well as external acts of obedience. The apostle Paul immediately emphasizes the inward attitude by quoting the Fifth Commandment: *"Honor* your father and mother" (v. 2, emphasis added).

Again, the *attitude* of honor and respect is a lifelong commitment, cultivated by a childhood and youth filled with *acts* of obedience.

The word translated "honor" in verse 2 is *timaō*. It signifies a reverent honor. In fact, it is the same Greek word used in John 5:23 to speak of reverence and honor toward God: "All men should honor the Son, even as they honor the Father." So it's a powerful word, suggesting that children should hold parents in awe and the deepest respect, so that there is a right attitude behind a right act, with the act of obedience always precipitated by an attitude of honor and reverential respect.

How important is obedience? We noted at the start of the chapter that the Fifth Commandment is the only one of the Ten

Commandments that is reinforced with a promise. It also sits at the head of the Second Table of the law. Have you noticed that it is also the only one of the ten that deals with how the family functions? That's because this is the foundation for all right relationships, both in the home and beyond. A home where children respect their parents will be a harmonious home. And a person who grows up with a sense of obedience, a sense of discipline, and a sense of respect toward his parents will be someone who can make any kind of human relationship work on any other level.

In other words, God's design is that all human relationships are based on what is learned through obedience in childhood. If children learn respect and submission in the family, that will enable them throughout life to have proper relationships. But if we raise a generation of undisciplined children who do not know what it is to respect authority, we will not only damage our children's relationships throughout life, but we will also help create a chaotic world.

To show how serious God was about this commandment, note that Exodus 21:15, Leviticus 20:9, and Deuteronomy 21:18–21 all require a sentence of death by stoning for incorrigible or violently rebellious children. One wonders what an impact it would have on the youth culture if our society enforced capital punishment against delinquent children. Most of the children's rights advocates in our culture want to outlaw spanking. If they only understood the implications of these verses, they would really be enraged!

But God commands children to obey, and He appoints parents to teach them obedience. This is one of the paramount goals of parenting: to produce obedient children. There is no more basic or essential task for any mom or dad.

HONORING THE LORD IN THE FAMILY

Look again at Ephesians 6:1: "Children, obey your parents *in the Lord.*" The phrase "in the Lord" means "for the Lord's sake." Puritan commentator Matthew Henry wrote, "Some take this as a limitation and understand it thus: 'as far as is consistent with your duty to God.' We must not disobey our heavenly Father in obedience to earthly parents; for our obligation to God is prior and superior to all others. I take it rather as a reason: 'Children, obey your parents; for the Lord has commanded it: obey them therefore for the Lord's sake, and with an eye to him.'"[1]

The Lord has placed parents over the child. Their authority derives from Him. Therefore when children rightly obey they do it as unto the Lord (cf. Colossians 3:23–24). In a sense, then, the parents stand in the place of the Lord, and children are to obey them "*in all things,* for this is well pleasing to the Lord" (v. 20, emphasis added).

The only exception would be if the parents command the child to do something evil. That is where obedience must stop. If the parents' commands are clearly in conflict with the revealed Word of God, "we ought to obey God rather than men" (Acts 5:29). All parents will make mistakes and at times be inconsistent, but that doesn't nullify their God-given authority. As children grow, there will undoubtedly be times when they disagree with their parents' instructions. But that doesn't nullify the child's responsibility to obey, either. Parents are accountable to God for their leadership; children are accountable to Him for their obedience.

Some parents do try to impose on their children behavior God has forbidden. I have known young people whose non-Christian parents have forbidden them to read their Bibles or even mention the name of Christ. Some unbelieving parents have tried to force their believing children to renounce Christ. In such cases, the child's duty is clearly to obey God rather than men.

But suppose a father instructs his son to mow the lawn on Saturday. Is the son entitled to disobey just because he believes God wants him to spend the day somewhere else? Not at all. "Obey[ing] God rather than men" is a matter of following His revealed Word, not some whimsical subjective feelings about what the Lord is leading us to do. God's clear instruction to the son at *this* point is in Ephesians 6:1: "Obey your parents." The son should mow the lawn. Only if the parents require the son to disobey God-breathed revelation—Scripture (2 Timothy 3:16)—is the son in a position where he must go against the parents' wishes.

And if God places a child in the position of having to disobey parents in order to obey Him, even that is not an excuse for a defiant, rebellious attitude. The child must willingly bear the consequences of disobeying his or her parents. I have known young people who were banished from their own families for the sake of their testimony for Christ. That is exactly what Jesus meant when He said, "I have come to 'set a man against his father, a daughter against her mother, and a daughter-in-law against her mother-in-law'; and 'a man's enemies will be those of his own household.' He who loves father or mother more than Me is not worthy of Me. And he who loves son or daughter more than Me is not worthy of Me" (Matthew 10:35–37).

Fortunately, it is very unusual, even in our God-hating society, for parents to persecute their children to such an extreme. The norm is that even in non-Christian families, children can and should obey their parents in *all* things, and they glorify God by doing so.

Why is God glorified when children submit to the authority of their parents? How does it glorify God even when a believing child submits to unbelieving parents? Ephesians 6:1: "For this is right." This is the way God has ordered the family, and it is simply *right* for children to obey their parents.

Someone will say, "But where is the psychological evidence? Who did the case studies? What are the child development experts' opinions about this?"

Does it matter what anyone else thinks? This is what *God* says: Obeying your parents is right. "The statutes of the Lord are right, rejoicing the heart" (Psalm 19:8). "All Your precepts concerning all things I consider to be right; I hate every false way" (Psalm 119:128). "Who is wise? Let him understand these things. Who is prudent? Let him know them. For the ways of the Lord are right; the righteous walk in them, but transgressors stumble in them" (Hosea 14:9).

We don't need a psychological survey. We don't need to investigate the theories of people who think differently. We don't need experts to lend credence to what Scripture says. God says this is right. And as Christians, our confidence in His precious Word is such that we regard the matter settled.

God is honored when children obey their parents, simply because this is what He has commanded.

DISCERNING THE ATTITUDE
BEHIND THE ACT

Notice that the focus of the Fifth Commandment is on the attitude, not merely the act, of obedience. The commandment itself doesn't even use the word "obey." It says, *"Honor* your father and mother" (Ephesians 6:2, emphasis added). That describes a heart disposition. It rules out reluctant obedience, angry obedience, or any show of obedience where the heart remains defiant. External compliance that veils an insubordinate heart is not God-honoring obedience. Merely external obedience is clearly not what is called for in Ephesians 6:1.

Honor is the attitude behind the act. Obedience without honor is nothing more than hypocrisy, and hypocrisy is a sin. This kind of hypocrisy is a sin that all children are prone to, and the wise parent will address not only *acts* of defiance, but wrong attitudes as well.

We can't judge the heart (1 Samuel 16:7), so how can parents know when the child's attitude is wrong? It's true that parents cannot always know a child's attitude with certainty, but there are certain telltale signs for which to look. Frankly, kids are usually not very subtle in displaying their attitudes. When the child complains and bellyaches, or displays a surly countenance, it is obvious that the attitude is wrong. Bitterness and displeasure are often revealed in grumbling murmurs and under-the-breath grousing. When parents observe such a demeanor in their children, they should address the issue of attitude.

My own children will testify that they were disciplined far more for their attitudes than for their actions. And we discovered that when parents deal with wrong attitudes, actions practically take care of themselves. We found that by catching defiance at the point of attitude, we were able to avert most defiant behavior.

What parents must do is pour the Word of God into their children so that it informs their conscience and it constantly talks to them. "For the word of God is living and powerful, and sharper than any two-edged sword, piercing even to the division of soul and spirit, and of joints and marrow, and is a discerner of the thoughts and intents of the heart" (Hebrews 4:12). Scripture "is profitable for doctrine, for reproof, for correction, for instruction in righteousness" (2 Timothy 3:16). And if the child's heart is stoked with Scripture, the child's own conscience will often rebuke wrong attitudes.

The conscience is a God-given warning system.[2] It's like a buzzer or a red light that signals when something is wrong. The conscience reacts to whatever moral values the mind has embraced. God graciously equips every child with a certain sense of right and wrong. That's what the apostle Paul spoke of in Romans 2:14–15 when he pointed out that even Gentiles have the law of God written in their hearts, and their conscience bears witness to it: "When Gentiles, who do not have the law, by nature do the things in the law, these, although not having the law, are a law to themselves, who show the work of the law written in their hearts, their conscience also bearing witness." In other words, everyone is born with some innate knowledge of right and wrong. To some degree, "what may be known of God is manifest in them" (Romans 1:19).

But left to themselves, people will inevitably suppress that law of God that is written in their hearts. They begin with an understanding of right and wrong; they just love wrong. They don't want to retain God in their knowledge (v. 28). And so they try by all means—rationalization, denial, or their own evil imaginations—to quell that God-given knowledge and inform their consciences with moral values more to their liking.

Secular culture has a negative effect as well, joining forces with an evil imagination to subvert the law of God in the heart and reconstruct the moral code that drives conscience.

Parents can combat this trend by helping fill the child's heart with Scripture. Memorization, family Bible study, and everyday conversation are all opportunities to instill biblical truth in the child's thinking. This, once again, is what Deuteronomy 6:7 instructs parents to do: "You shall teach [these words] diligently to your children, and shall talk of them when you sit in your house, when you walk by the way, when you lie down, and when you rise up."

And a mind and conscience driven by the Word of God becomes a fountain for right attitudes.

In many ways, the attitude of obedience is much more vital than the act, because if the attitude is right, the act will naturally follow. But the right action with the wrong attitude is nothing but hypocrisy. The child guilty of such hypocrisy is not truly honoring his or her parents.

We noted above that the Greek word translated "honor" speaks of an esteem that amounts to reverence. Children are to venerate their parents—that is, hold them in such high admiration and respect that they regard them with a sense of awe.

But the word "honor" can also mean something else. In 1 Timothy 5:17, the apostle Paul uses the same Greek word for "honor": "Let the elders who rule well be counted worthy of double honor, especially those who labor in the word and doctrine." That is speaking about financial support. Elders who rule well are worthy of double pay. Verse 18 makes the meaning unmistakable: "For the Scripture says, 'You shall not muzzle an ox while it treads out the grain,' and, 'The laborer is worthy of his wages.'"

Honoring one's parents is, first of all, an attitude, but true honor also involves a willingness to take care of them when they have needs. Our parents give us all we need in the first couple of decades of our lives. The time eventually comes for most families when the children need to help support the parents.

This was the very issue Jesus took up with the Pharisees in Matthew 15:4–8: "God commanded, saying, 'Honor your father and your mother'; and, 'He who curses father or mother, let him be put to death.' But you say, 'Whoever says to his father or mother, "Whatever profit you might have received from me is a gift to God"; then he need not honor his father or mother.' Thus you have made the commandment of God of no effect by your tradition. Hypocrites! Well did Isaiah prophesy about you, saying: 'These people draw near to Me with their mouth, And honor Me with their lips, but their heart is far from Me.'"

Notice that underlying their refusal to provide for the needs of their parents was an attitude of hypocrisy, and that was where Jesus aimed His rebuke.

Children whose *attitudes* are right—whose honor for their parents comes from the heart—will retain that deep respect and love for their parents throughout life. I cherish the thought that someday if my parents come to a point in life when they have needs I can supply, I will be able to return some of the loving care they showed to me when I was growing up. That is part of honor. That is the way God designed the family to be.

But it all hinges on the right attitude. And woe to the parent who is concerned with the child's actions but fails to address the attitude.

PROFITING FROM THE PROMISE

Let's examine the promise that accompanies the Fifth Commandment: "That it may be well with you and you may live long on the earth" (Ephesians 6:3). Again, this is the only one of the Ten Commandments that is accompanied by a promised blessing to those who obey. This commandment, because it is the key to all human relationships, is so vital that God Himself underscored it by the inclusion of this promise.

There are two aspects to the promise: "That it may be well with you." That promises *quality* of life. "And you may live long on the earth." That promises *quantity* of life. Those who honor their parents tend to live fuller, longer lives than those who grow up defiant.

Some would confine this promise to Old Testament Israel, because as the earthly nation through whom God would raise up the family line of the Messiah, they were the recipients of many tangible, earthly, physical promises that do not apply literally to Christians (e.g., Genesis 13:15; Ezekiel 37:21–28). But the apostle Paul cites *this* promise as applying to New Testament believers as well.

Is this promise an ironclad guarantee? Does it mean that the reward for submission to one's parents is *always* a long and rich life? No. Some who obey and honor their parents do die at a young age. But all exceptions to the rule aside, it is certainly true that obedience results in a longer, more harmonious life, and a defiant attitude always causes misery, and often causes people to die before their time.

In other words, submission to parents is in the child's own best interest. It is not only *right* in God's eyes (Ephesians 6:1), it is also best for the child. Obedience will keep the child from a world of harm. A right attitude of submission and respect will save him from a lifetime of bitterness, anger, and resentment. It will generally prolong life, and it will surely make the years of anyone's life fuller and richer.

Six

The Nurture and Admonition of the Lord

*And you, fathers, do not provoke your children to wrath,
but bring them up in the training and admonition of the Lord.*

—EPHESIANS 6:4

Six

❧❦❧

The Nurture and Admonition of the Lord

The children's duty in the home is to obey. The flip side is the *parents'* duty: to teach them that obedience in an environment of godly nurturing, without exasperating them in the process.

It's a tall order. This doesn't come naturally for parents, any more than obedience comes naturally for kids.

We've talked a lot about the effect of human depravity on the child. But let's remember that parents are depraved, too. Our own natural inclinations are bent toward sin, just as our children's are. *Christian* parents have a tremendous advantage, because as redeemed people they have regenerate hearts. They have godly desires and righteous appetites. Unlike unregenerate people, they are capable of truly loving God, and, in fact, love for God is the driving passion that distinguishes a true Christian (Romans 8:28; 1 John 5:2).

Nonetheless, even Christian parents still struggle with the remnants of fleshly appetites and ungodly habits. Like the apostle Paul, we often find ourselves doing the very things we hate (Romans 7:15–24).

We are all too prone to fleshly and sinful behavior, and this has its inevitable effect on our parenting.

As we noted in the previous chapter, God has assigned parents authority over their children, and He has commanded children to obey their parents in "all things" (Colossians 3:20). That does not mean, however, that parents are automatically always right. There are times when parents permit their own sinful attitudes and actions to surface in their parenting. When we do that, it exasperates the child. And God solemnly warns parents not to let this happen.

"And you, fathers, do not provoke your children to wrath, but bring them up in the training and admonition of the Lord" (Ephesians 6:4). The same commandment is echoed in Colossians 3:21, "Fathers, provoke not your children to anger, lest they be discouraged."

Our first impression, reading this in English, is that it is addressed to fathers in particular, perhaps because they are the head of the home, or perhaps because fathers have a greater tendency than mothers to exasperate children. But a closer look reveals that this commandment is not necessarily addressing fathers alone. The word translated "fathers" in Ephesians 6:4 is *patera,* which *can* refer to fathers in particular but is often used to speak of both parents. Hebrews 11:23, for example, says, "By faith Moses, when he was born, was hidden three months by his *[patera].*" There the word clearly refers to both parents. I'm convinced Ephesians 6:4 is using *patera* in a similar way, encompassing mother and father alike. Certainly, the *principle* in this verse applies equally to both parents. And the *responsibilities* of nurture, training, and admonition clearly pertain to mothers as well as to fathers. So this command applies to *parents,* not merely fathers.

In Paul's day, Ephesians 6:4 literally confronted the whole social order. Families were presided over by fathers (not parents), and fathers could do whatever they pleased in the context of their families, without compunction or social stigma. No Roman father ever felt the duty to avoid provoking his children's wrath. The responsibility lay only with children not to provoke their *father's* wrath, and if they did, the consequences could be severe.

Rome had a law called *patria potestas* ("the father's power"). This principle gave men who were full Roman citizens absolute property rights over their own families. The children, the wife, and even the slaves were regarded as the patriarch's personal chattel, and he could do with them as he wished. By law, he had full authority to dispose of all family matters, or family *members*, in whatever way pleased him.

In effect, then, *patria potestas* also gave the patriarch absolute authority over every area of his children's lives. Fathers arranged marriages for their children. They could also force them to divorce. A displeased father could disown his children, sell them into slavery, or even kill them if he wished—all without resorting to a court of law.

When a child was born, the child was placed between the father's feet. If the father picked up the child, the child stayed in the home. If the father turned and walked away, the child was either left to die or taken to the forum and sold at auction. Most children auctioned away at birth were raised to work as prostitutes or slaves.

A Roman man named Hilary wrote this letter to his wife, Alis, sometime in the first century B.C.: "Heartiest greetings. Note that we are still even now in Alexandria. Do not worry, if when all others return, I remain in Alexandria. I beg and beseech you to take care of the little child, and as soon as we receive wages, I will send them to you. If—good luck to you—you have another child, if it is a boy, let it live; if it is a girl, expose it [throw it away]."[1]

Seneca, a contemporary of the apostle Paul's, described Roman policy with regard to unwanted animals: "We slaughter a fierce ox; we strangle a mad dog; we plunge a knife into a sick cow. Children born weak or deformed we drown." Such was the state of society's attitude toward children in the apostle Paul's time.

Things are frankly no better, and may even be worse, in our culture. Millions of unwanted babies are aborted each year. And statistics show that most children in foster homes in America are not there because they are orphans or because their families are financially destitute. Most are there simply because their parents did not want them. Children have become a disposable commodity in our society, just as they were in ancient Rome.

The Bible calls Christian parents to a different standard. It was a revolutionary standard in the apostle Paul's day, and it still runs counter to society's values in our day. Scripture does not give fathers dictatorial power over their children. Children are not to be regarded as property of the parents. Instead, Scripture speaks to parents as stewards of the Lord, responsible to provide a proper nurturing environment for children, whom the Lord has graciously placed into their care. Like all stewards, parents will ultimately give account for how they have fulfilled their stewardship. And the primary standards by which our parenting will be judged are what Paul sets forth in Ephesians 6:4.

What are the specific duties the apostle Paul outlines in this crucial verse? I see the following three.

DON'T PROVOKE THEM TO ANGER

"[Parents], do not provoke your children to wrath," Paul writes. This is a caution, a warning, designed to put parents on guard against stirring their children's anger either deliberately or through careless but unnecessary provocations.

There are times, of course, when children become sinfully angry with their parents apart from any provocation. The child's own selfishness, immaturity, or wrong attitudes might be the cause of the anger. In such cases, it is the child who is sinning.

But there are other times when the parents are guilty of provoking their children's anger by thoughtlessly aggravating them, by deliberately goading them, by callously neglecting them, or by any number of other intentional or careless means that exasperate them. When that happens, it is the parents who are sinning—and provoking the child to sin as well.

Remember that our children are commanded by God to honor us. Therefore when parents provoke their own children to wrath, they are causing them to sin against the Fifth Commandment. In such cases the parent is not only guilty before God for disobeying Ephesians 6:4, he or she is also doubly guilty for causing the child to stumble. This is an extremely destructive sin.

Christian parents who goad their children to anger, or fail to give them the nurture and admonition of the Lord, forfeit all the benefits of a distinctively Christian family. Virtually no environment is more unwholesome for a child than a nominally Christian family where parents invoke the name of the Lord but neglect to provide the proper loving nurture and admonition. Many children from such "Christian" families end up more hostile to the things of the Lord than kids who have grown up in utterly pagan surroundings. Christian parents who neglect Ephesians 6:4 will reap what they have sown—pain and heartache equal to or surpassing that of worldly families.

The Greek word translated "provoke" is *parorgizō*, meaning, "to anger" or "to enrage." It might describe a lashing, open rebellion; or it could also refer to an internal smoldering and a seething, secret vexation. Both kinds of wrath are commonly seen in children whose parents have provoked them.

How do parents make their children angry? There are many ways to do this. Here are some of the common ones:

Overprotection

You can anger your children by fencing them in too much. Smothering them. Never trusting them. Always assuming they are not telling you the truth. Never giving them an opportunity to develop independence, thus making them feel stifled and crushed.

This is a particular danger in today's world. Parents certainly need to protect their children, especially in an environment with so many dangers. When I was a child I could freely roam our neighborhood. I could get on my bike and ride around in relative safety. Unfortunately, the world today is a lot more hazardous than it was when I was a child, and many parents live in neighborhoods where they simply cannot give their children that much freedom.

But overprotection poses a danger, too. Remember Laban in the Old Testament? He was an overprotective, domineering parent. He dealt dishonestly with Jacob to get him to marry Leah, Laban's eldest daughter, even though Jacob loved Rachel, the younger one. Laban then permitted Jacob to marry Rachel, too, in exchange for a promise that Jacob would stay and work for Laban for seven years (Genesis 29:26). When the time came for Jacob to move on, Laban begged them to stay (30:25–27). His overprotective parenting, and his subsequent meddling in his son-in-law's marriage, cost his own daughters a healthy marriage.

Ironically, despite Laban's overprotective meddling in his daughters' affairs, the daughters' assessment was that their father did not truly care for them, that he counted them as strangers and had devoured their rightful inheritance (31:14–17). What he, no doubt, thought of as an expression of parental attachment came across to them as evidence that he did not really love them.

Parents who smother their children with overprotection often convince themselves that they are acting in the child's best interest. But it is a sure way to provoke a child to anger. Overprotection communicates a lack of trust in the child. Children over sheltered by their parents begin to despair of ever earning the parents' trust. They may even conclude that how they behave is irrelevant. Rules and restrictions without privileges become a suffocating prison. Many who cannot abide such confinement finally rebel.

Children need some degree of freedom and independence in order to grow, to learn, and to make their own mistakes. They will never learn to handle responsibility unless they are given a degree of liberty. Mothers who tie their children to their apron-strings are merely fostering resentment. And fathers who refuse to give their children breathing room will exasperate their children in exactly the way Ephesians 6:4 forbids.

Overindulgence

The flip side of overprotection is overindulgence. Excessively permissive parents—parents who spoil their children—are as likely to stir their children's wrath as those who smother them.

Studies prove that children given too much freedom begin to feel insecure and unloved. And why not? Scripture clearly says, "He who spares his rod hates his son" (Proverbs 13:24). Parents who indulge or coddle their misbehaving children are actually displaying unloving behavior toward them. Is it any wonder that the children sense this and become exasperated?

Our society has fostered increasingly permissive attitudes toward children for many years. We are now reaping the harvest of a whole generation of angry young people.

Favoritism

A third sure-fire way to provoke anger in our children is by showing favoritism among siblings. Isaac favored Esau over Jacob, and Rebecca preferred Jacob over Esau (Genesis 25:28). Remember what terrible agony resulted in that family? Esau and Jacob became bitter rivals. Jacob repeatedly used trickery and deceit to try to eclipse his brother and vie for his father's blessing. He lured Esau into bartering away his birthright, and he ultimately beguiled Isaac, with Rebecca's help, into giving Jacob the blessing Isaac meant for Esau. The resulting tension literally split the family, and Jacob had to flee for his life from his brother (Genesis 27).

Nonetheless, the tendency toward favoritism spilled over into the next generation as well. Jacob's best-beloved son was Joseph, whom he favored with a many-colored coat. That provoked such jealousy in the other brothers that they conspired to kill Joseph. They ended up selling him into slavery instead. And thus another generation of that family was torn apart. Though God ultimately used it all for good, the favoritism itself, and all the jealousies it provoked, were entirely evil, and they bore much evil fruit.

Don't make the error of favoritism with your children. Don't give gifts or privileges to one that you withhold from another. Don't even compare your children with one other. Don't say things like, "Why can't you be like your brother?" Don't use one child's virtues or talents as the standard against which to measure another's performance. There's nothing more humiliating for a child than to be demeaned or debased by an unkind comparison to a sibling or classmate.

You really want to destroy a young child? Just make him feel inferior to everyone else in the family. Portray him as the black sheep of the family. You will saddle him with a terrible sense of frustration, and you will provoke him to wrath in the process.

Unrealistic Goals

Many parents provoke their children to wrath by constantly pushing achievement. Pressure your child to fulfill goals you never accomplished, and you'll destroy the child.

It is certainly every parents' responsibility to encourage and prompt their children to higher levels of achievement. In 1 Thessalonians 2:11 the apostle Paul reminded the Thessalonians of his fatherly concern for them: "We exhorted, and comforted, and charged every one of you, as a father does his own children." The exhortations and the fatherly charges certainly have their place, but notice that they are to be balanced by loving comfort. Parents who only push their children to achieve more, without comforting them in the midst of their failures, are goading their children to resentment.

Push your children to unrealistic or unrealizable goals and you will rob your child of any sense of fulfillment. When my sons were young and playing organized sports, it seemed every team they ever played on had at least one father who had brow-beaten his son so much that the child lived in fear of failure and therefore did not play up to his potential. I have known many parents who kept unrelenting pressure on their children to achieve higher grades. Most such parents are motivated by sheer selfishness. They are merely trying to fulfill their own unrealized childhood goals through their kids. That's an unfair burden to place on any child.

One beautiful teenage girl I knew was literally driven insane by pressure from her parents. I visited her in a padded cell where she lay in a catatonic state, motionless except for a constant trembling. She had been a top-notch student, a cheerleader, and a homecoming princess. But it was never enough for her parents. Her mother, in particular, kept constant pressure on her to achieve more, look better, and act differently. Everything she did was an occasion for her mother to tell her how she might have done it better. And under so much pressure, she finally cracked. After several weeks of rest and medical treatment, she recovered to the point where she no longer needed to be institutionalized. Finally, she was sent home—right back into the pressure-cooker environment her mother had made of her home life. A short time later she took her own life. Why? Her words to me sometime before her final breakdown: "No matter what I do, it never satisfies my mother." Believe me, that young woman had achieved far beyond her mother's own potential, but the mother was trying to live out her own fantasies through that daughter. What a tragedy! She goaded her daughter into a self-destructive rage.

Discouragement

In a similar vein, you can provoke a child to wrath by discouraging him. Remember the parallel verse in Colossians 3:21, which says, "Fathers, provoke not your children to anger, *lest they be discouraged*" (emphasis added). Avoiding discouragement is the whole thrust of this commandment.

Parents provoke their children to anger when they constantly criticize them but never reward them, never praise their accomplishments, and never allow them to enjoy their own successes. A child who feels he can never get his parents' approval will soon give up trying to earn it at all. There may be no quicker way to provoke your children to wrath than by perpetually discouraging them.

This is easy to do. Always focus on what they do wrong, and never notice what they do right. Always notice their faults, but never say anything about their positive qualities. Ignore their natural gifts and talents, and harp on the things they don't do well. Be constantly suspicious of them.

I had a simple rule of thumb in raising my children: For every time I had to point out to them something that was wrong, I tried to equalize it soon thereafter by pointing out something they had done right. It wasn't always easy. ("I like the way you've arranged your drawer.") But a loving parent can always find *something* as a source of encouragement. And every child responds well to encouragement and approval.

I remember what it was like as a child to feel I could sit at the table a hundred times and *not* spill a glass of milk, but no one ever noticed *that*. Spill something one time, however, and it would not go unnoticed. Parents, make it a point to notice when your kids do well, as much or more than you notice when they don't.

Haim Ginott wrote, "A child learns what he lives. If he lives with criticism he does not learn responsibility. He learns to condemn himself and to find fault with others. He learns to doubt his own judgment, to disparage his own ability, and to distrust the intentions of others. And above all, he learns to live with continual expectation of impending doom."[2] Raise your children like that and you are certain to provoke their wrath.

Neglect

Another way to provoke your children to wrath is through neglect. Fail to show them affection. Show them indifference instead. Don't take an interest in what interests them. Don't be concerned for their needs. You will stir the wrath of your child.

The classic biblical example of a neglected child is Absalom. Though David was by no means indifferent to his son (2 Samuel 18:33), he *treated* him with indifference, and Absalom grew up with a contempt for his own father. He murdered his own brother (13:28–29). He deliberately undermined David's kingly authority (15:1–6). He plotted David's overthrow (15:10). He defiled his father's wives in the sight of all Israel (16:22). When the full tab came due for David's fatherly neglect, it ultimately included rebellion, civil war, and finally Absalom's death.

Many parents communicate a similar neglect by treating their kids as an intrusion. Too many children overhear their parents say things like, "Well, we'd love to go with you, Albert, but we've got these kids. And we can't get anybody to stay with them. It's this way all the time." If you want to exasperate your children, simply make them feel unwanted. Make them feel as if they're standing in the way of things you'd like to do. Act as if you resent them, and they will begin to resent you.

I made an arrangement with my sons, Matt and Mark, when they were growing up. I went to their games, and they came to my sermons. It worked marvelously. I did not neglect them, and they did not neglect me.

I had a friend in the ministry who traveled around the country speaking to youth groups. He was on the road a lot, and between speaking engagements he often came home for just a day or two. While he was home once, he overheard his little boy talking across the fence to the boy next door.

"Hey," the little boy said to his pal, "can you play catch?"

"No," was the reply. "I'm going to play catch with my dad."

Then my friend heard his own little boy reply, "Oh. My dad

doesn't have time to play with me. He's too busy playing with other people's kids."

My friend wisely changed his ministry so he would have more time to spend with his son.

In many ways neglect is the worst kind of child abuse. Our streets and cities are filled with neglected children, and virtually all of them are angry. Their parents bear much of the responsibility for that.

Condescension

You will provoke your children to wrath if you refuse to allow them to grow up. If you put them down or laugh at them when they say naïve or immature things; if you constantly talk down to them; or if you stifle them every time they want to try something you think is too grown up for them, you will never encourage them to grow, and you will actually confirm them in their immaturity.

The apostle Paul said, "When I was a child, I spoke as a child, I understood as a child, I thought as a child; but when I became a man, I put away childish things" (1 Corinthians 13:11). That's the natural course of the maturing process. Parents should encourage their children in that pursuit, not extinguish the child's enthusiasm for growth. Don't treat them condescendingly; encourage their growth. Let them make some mistakes without getting hammered.

When my son Matt was a toddler, he once flushed my watch down a toilet. I asked him, "Why did you do that?"

He looked at me with solemn eyes. "I just wanted to see what it would look like going down," he said.

Did I punish him severely? No. *I'd* like to have seen what it looked like going down, too. I remember being that age.

Sometimes kids say childish and funny things, and it is natural for parents to enjoy the humor of such situations. But be careful not to crush your child in the process. Don't laugh in his face. Don't belittle him for his natural childishness. Usually if you must laugh, it's better to laugh later. In the meantime, while they grope their way through the maturing process, give them encouragement and support and confidence. Let them present their ridiculous ideas. Let them experiment with thinking for themselves. Otherwise you will discourage and aggravate them in the very way the apostle Paul cautions parents against.

Withdrawing Love

Don't employ affection as a tool of reward and punishment. I cringe when I overhear a parent say, "Mommy won't like you if you do that." Sometimes parents do this unconsciously, by behavior that suggests they care less for the child when he disobeys. They might also send a similar message subliminally when they praise their children with words like, "That's such a good little girl! Mommy *loves* you when you're so good."

Scripture says love "bears all things, believes all things, hopes all things, endures all things. Love never fails" (1 Corinthians 13:7–8). Real love doesn't rise or fall based on the achievements or failures of love's object. Does God's love for us fail when we fail Him? Not at all. In fact, "God demonstrate[d] His own love toward us, in that *while we were still sinners,* Christ died for us" (Romans 5:8). In other words, the greatest expression of God's love toward us was that He sacrificed His beloved son to atone for our sins and reconcile us to Himself, while we were still in a state of utter enmity against Him (v. 10).

Parents must model the same kind of love for their children. Threatening to withdraw our love when they misbehave undermines love itself, and it provokes our children to anger.

Excessive Discipline

Too much chastisement is another guaranteed way to provoke a child to anger. Some parents seem to have the opinion that if discipline is good for a child, an abundance of discipline must be *really* good for them. They ride their kids constantly, holding the threat of corporal punishment over their heads like an unrelenting sword of Damocles.

Such behavior is really nothing but brutality. The father who throws his weight around, or uses superior strength—whether physically or verbally—can be devastating to a child's spirit. It's easy for grownups to do, because they are physically, intellectually, and verbally so much more skilled than a child. But parents who treat little children that way will reap the whirlwind when kids reach their middle teenage years. Kids who have been bullied will grow up with a mean streak themselves, their wrath provoked by their parents' own unkindness.

I'm amazed at how easily some parents use hurtful words in rebuking their children. They say things to their kids they would never say to anyone else—things that would crush a sensitive child's heart, and would goad *any* child to wrath.

Scripture says that God always disciplines His children in love (Hebrews 12:5–7). The writer of Hebrews seems to acknowledge that human parents are all too prone to discipline their children capriciously or erratically: "Furthermore we have had fathers of our flesh which corrected us, and we gave them reverence: shall we not much rather be in subjection unto the Father of spirits, and live? For they verily for a few days chastened us after their own pleasure; but he for our profit, that we might be partakers of his holiness" (vv. 9–10, KJV).

Unfortunately, human parents do sometimes tend to discipline children selfishly or impulsively, but God's discipline is always for our good. Christian parents should strive to make the child's own interests the goal of all our discipline. If we do that, we minimize the risk of perturbing and exasperating them unnecessarily.

So that's the negative side of Paul's instructions to parents: Don't exasperate your children. What about the positive side? "Bring them up in the training and admonition of the Lord" (Ephesians 6:4). Notice the two aspects of that: training and admonition. We'll examine the training aspect first.

GIVE THEM THE RIGHT TRAINING

The Greek word translated "training" is *paideia,* from the Greek word for "child," *pais. Paideia* means "tutorage, instruction, nurture." The same word is used once in 2 Timothy 3:16, where it is translated "instruction," and four times in Hebrews 12:5–11, where it is translated "chastening." So the notions of chastening and discipline, as well as positive instruction, are inherent in the word *paideia.* Many people automatically think of corporal punishment when terms like "discipline" and "chastening" are brought up. And corporal punishment would certainly be included in all that is meant by *paideia.* We'll set that topic aside for the moment, however, and take it up in our discussion of the word "admonition" below.

Meanwhile, much more than corporal punishment is encompassed in the word *paideia.* It is a comprehensive word describing all aspects of child training—guidance, instruction, and both positive and negative discipline. The King James Version translates the word as "nurture" in Ephesians 6:4. I like that translation. I think it captures the gist of the loving instruction and care that Paul is calling for in this verse.

Note the words "bring them up." We must *bring* our children up. They will not get there themselves. This has been one of our recurring themes in this book. Parents must take an active role in shaping the characters of their children. Proverbs 29:15 says, "A child left to himself brings shame to his mother." Again, what ruins most children is not what their parents *do to them,* but what they *do not do for them.*

The real key to the challenging work of bringing up our children correctly is to create an environment of nurture and loving instruction in which their hearts become fertile grounds for God's truth. It is the child's *heart* that parents are to nurture.

Proverbs 4:23 says, "Keep your heart with all diligence, for out of it spring the issues of life." All the matters of life proceed from the heart. Jesus said, "For from within, out of the heart of men, proceed evil thoughts, adulteries, fornications, murders, thefts, covetousness, wickedness, deceit, lewdness, an evil eye, blasphemy, pride, foolishness. All these evil things come from within and defile a man" (Mark 7:21–23). A similar saying is recorded in Luke 6:45: "A good man out of the good treasure of his heart brings forth good; and an evil man out of the evil treasure of his heart brings forth evil. For out of the abundance of the heart his mouth speaks." Whatever fills your heart will determine what your mouth speaks.

Parents must realize this and nurture the child's heart. The child's depravity is a heart problem. When we deal with misbehavior, it is not primarily a behavioral issue. Rather, the misconduct reflects the fallenness of the child's heart.

In fact, parents should be very clear about this: Behavior is *not* the crucial issue. A change in behavior will not fix the child's root problem. As we have emphasized repeatedly, a change in behavior without a change in heart is nothing but hypocrisy.

How can parents nurture the child's heart? To begin with, parents need to help the children understand that they have sinful hearts. Children themselves need to know that all their evil words, thoughts, and deeds spring from sin-tainted hearts, and the only remedy for this is the gospel (see chapter three). In other words, keep the children's own heart-needs always in their (as well as the parents') focus, so that your children never lose sight of this fact: Not only is regeneration their greatest need; it is also your greatest concern as a parent. Ted Tripp has written a marvelous book for parents titled *Shepherding a Child's Heart*,[3] in which he offers much helpful advice on how to maintain the proper focus in our parenting. He suggests that the child's heart is the world's smallest battlefield, and the conquering of it calls for all-out, hand-to-hand combat.[4]

He's right. Your child's heart is a battlefield where sin and righteousness are in conflict. Your child's *greatest* problem is not a lack of maturity. It is not a lack of experience or a lack of understanding. It is a wicked heart. Those other things will exacerbate the heart problem. But the remedies for immaturity, ignorance, and inexperience are no cure for the main problem. Your child will not *outgrow* his own depravity.

As parents, we must target the children's hearts. We cannot merely target behavior, or our parenting will be shallow and superficial, and we will raise our children to be spiritually shallow.

The goal of parenting is not behavior control. It is not merely to produce well-mannered children. It is not to teach our kids socially commendable behavior. It is not to make them polite and respectful. It is not to make them obedient. It is not to get them to perform for our approval. It is not to conform them to a moral standard. It is not to give us, as parents, something to be proud of.

The ultimate goal and proper focus of biblical parenting is redemptive. Parents are responsible to lead their children to Christ. As we have emphasized previously, parents are not capable of *guaranteeing* their children's conversion. Parents cannot obtain salvation on their children's behalf. But from the time children are born until there is fruit that indicates they have been born again, parents are in the role of evangelists, constantly pointing and urging their children toward Christ, who alone can remedy the heart problems that cause them to love unrighteousness.

Any objective less than that is merely behavior modification. Frankly, non-Christian children can be made to conform to an external moral standard. All kids can be taught obedience to their parents. We know from all that we have studied so far that teaching our kids those things is a vital *part* of the parents' duty. *But those things are not to be confused with the main goal.*

Don't just teach your children external self-control; train them to understand temptation and resist it. Don't just teach them manners; teach them why pride is sinful and why greed, lust, selfishness, and covetousness dishonor God. Punish them for external offenses, but teach them that the *root* issue is always a deeper problem—corruption in their hearts. When you correct them, don't do it merely to satisfy you as the offended, irritated, frustrated parent. That's anger; it's vengeance. But when you correct them, help them to see that it is first of all *God* who has been offended and that He offers reconciliation through Jesus Christ (2 Corinthians 5:20).

As we have stressed repeatedly, this involves teaching them the whole counsel of God. It involves "doctrine . . . reproof . . . correction . . . instruction in righteousness" (2 Timothy 3:16). But its proper focus is, first of all, redemption. We have not achieved much if we merely teach unregenerate children to conform to a behavioral standard. As Ted Tripp writes, "A change in behavior that does not stem from a change in the heart is not commendable; it is *condemnable.*"[5]

A passage we keep returning to is Deuteronomy 6:6–7: "And these words which I command you today shall be in your heart.

You shall teach them diligently to your children, and shall talk of them when you sit in your house, when you walk by the way, when you lie down, and when you rise up." That defines the parenting responsibility. Notice that the proper focus begins with the *parent's* heart: "These words . . . shall be in *your heart.*" Parents whose own hearts are cold and devoid of the Word of God cannot properly shepherd their own children's hearts.

Now notice how beautifully the context of this commandment sets forth the parents' whole agenda, beginning with the familiar words of verse four: "Hear, O Israel: The LORD our God, the LORD is one!" Here is the parent's first task: *Teach your children about God.*

Verse five is also a familiar commandment. Jesus called it the first and great commandment: "You shall love the LORD your God with all your heart, with all your soul, and with all your strength." This is the second stage of parental instruction: *Teach them to love God.*

Stage three is a corollary: *Teach them to obey God from the heart.* "And these words which I command you today shall be in your heart. You shall teach them diligently to your children" (vv. 6–7). The "words" this refers to are the inspired words of God and the law in particular. The inescapable implication is that we are to teach our children about obedience to God from the heart.

Fourth, *teach them to follow your example.* "Teach them diligently to your children, and talk of them when you sit in your house, when you walk by the way, when you lie down, and when you rise up. You shall bind them as a sign on your hand, and they shall be as frontlets between your eyes" (vv. 7–8). In other words, show your children that the Word of the living God is always on the tip of your tongue, at all times in your life and in every experience of your life. Let them see that your life is dominated by divine truth. Let them see all of life as a classroom. View every occasion in life as an opportunity to teach them about God. Take every opportunity to point them to heaven. Make everything that happens a path that leads them back to Scripture.

Jesus was the absolute master at this kind of teaching. He drew spiritual lessons from all the world around Him. Water, fig trees, mustard seeds, birds, bread, grapes, pearls, wheat and tares, cups and platters, men and women, light and dark, nets, dinners, vineyards, foxes—everything in life opened up a window into divine truth. All parents are called to a similar teaching style with their children. Every flower, every rock, every mountain, the ocean, the sky, the cricket's chirp, the roaring waterfall, little babies, a puppy, a squirrel, and on and on—all these things make a well-equipped classroom to teach them truth about God, and to envelop them in the nurture of His truth.

Pay attention to the language of verse eight: "Bind them as a sign on your hand, and they shall be as frontlets between your eyes." That is simply a way of saying parents must keep the Word of God perpetually at the front of our minds, and always at hand. Verse nine continues, "You shall write them on the doorposts of your house and on your gates." In other words, make these truths the distinguishing mark of your home. Those expressions aren't literally meant to prescribe phylacteries (amulets containing scraps of Scripture bound to the forehead and hands by leather straps) or mezuzahs (boxes with Scripture verses nailed to the doorposts). Instead, they are charging parents with the responsibility of making the truth of Scripture the very focus of the household.

Here's another lesson from Deuteronomy 6: *Teach them to be wary of the world around them.* Verses 10–12 say, "So it shall be, when the LORD your God brings you into the land of which He swore to your fathers, to Abraham, Isaac, and Jacob, to give you large and beautiful cities which you did not build, houses full of all good things, which you did not fill, hewn-out wells which you did not dig, vineyards and olive trees which you did not plant; when you have eaten and are full; then beware, lest you forget the LORD who brought you out of the land of Egypt, from the house of bondage."

Parents need to prepare their children for life in a world full of temptations, idols, and even *good* things that can distract their hearts from the true God. They must not forget the Lord.

All of that and more is encompassed in the word *paideia,* "instruction" or "nurture" (KJV). Nurture your children in an environment like that, targeting their hearts with the truth of God's Word, and you will be providing the kind of instruction Paul calls for in Ephesians 6:4.

ADMONISH THEM WHEN NECESSARY

The other word Paul uses in this verse is "admonition" or *nouthesia* in the Greek text. It's a word that speaks of a rebuke or a warning. But it also conveys the sense of a mild, loving parental admonition. It's virtually a synonym of *paideia,* rather than a contrasting term. Both words include the connotation of parental discipline and chastisement.

Here we revisit a subject that we introduced in chapter four— corporal punishment. The subject is inexplicably baffling to many parents. Part of the problem is the confusion of the times in which we live. It has been popular for more than half a century to decry corporal punishment as inherently inappropriate, counterproductive, and detrimental to the child. A group of researchers studying corporal punishment summed up their perspective this way: "We suggest that reduction or elimination of corporal punishment could have major benefits for children and for reducing antisocial behavior in society."[6] Psychologist, mother, and well-known anti-spanking activist Penelope Leach distills the typical humanist perspective on corporal punishment: "I am a part of that non-spanking group, both as a mother and as a psychologist. I believe that spanking—or tapping, or slapping, or cuffing, or shaking, or beating, or whipping—children is actually wrong. I also believe . . . that far from producing better disciplined people, spanking makes it much more difficult to teach children how to behave."[7] Notice how she equates spanking with slapping, cuffing, shaking, beating, whipping, and, inexplicably, tapping. But those are not all the same thing, and they should not be likened to the rod of discipline administered in love.

Opponents of corporal punishment will often cite surveys and statistics that seem to support their findings, but precisely because they *begin* by equating brutal acts of violence against children with properly administered corporal discipline, their results are skewed. *Of course* cruel punishment and brute violence against children is wrong, counterproductive, and unbiblical.

But as we noted in an earlier chapter, Scripture does nonetheless prescribe the rod of discipline as a *necessary* aspect of parenting. In fact, Scripture flatly contradicts modern opponents of corporal punishment: "He who spares his rod hates his son, but he who loves him disciplines him promptly" (Proverbs 13:24). "Foolishness is bound up in the heart of a child; the rod of correction will drive it far from him" (22:15). "You shall beat him with a rod, and deliver his soul from hell" (23:14).

Moreover, according to a recent article in *U.S. News and World Report*,[8] "parenting experts" have based all their findings against corporal punishment "on a body of research that is at best inconclusive and at worst badly flawed."[9] According to the article, some recent studies indicate that spanking, when used appropriately, does indeed make children "less likely to fight with others and more likely to obey their parents." And there is also evidence to suggest that child-care psychologists and the news media have deliberately suppressed researchers' findings that argue in favor of corporal punishment. One "expert," confronted with evidence that calls the anti-spanking perspective into question, said, "There's enough evidence to decide we don't need [spanking] . . . even if the evidence isn't that strong."[10]

However, one study on spanking that began by eliminating examples of actual *abuse* (punishment where parents bruised or injured their children), found that non-abusive spanking does actually benefit the child more than alternative forms of discipline. In one very thorough study, Psychologist Robert E. Larzelere, director of residential research at Boys Town in Nebraska, failed to find any convincing evidence that nonabusive spanking, as typically used by parents, damaged children. Even more surprisingly, Larzelere's review revealed that no other discipline technique, including timeout and withdrawal of privileges, had more beneficial results for children under thirteen than spanking, in terms of getting children to comply with their parents' wishes.[11] But the article also concludes that the secular parenting experts' public stance against corporal punishment is not going to change anytime soon.

Naturally, no child-development specialist is about to run out to write a book called *Why You Should Spank Your Child,* which may be one reason why the news media have buried the notion that spanking might in some cases be a useful discipline technique. After ethicist Kevin Ryan, director of the Center for the Advancement of Ethics and Character at Boston University, was quoted in the *New York Times* a few years ago saying, "Mild physical punishment is appropriate in extreme cases." He says, "I never got so much hate mail about anything."[12]

Many who oppose corporal punishment simply are not willing to look at the facts and statistics rationally. One critic of spanking bluntly states that as far as he is concerned, "Hitting children is not a subject to which rational debate applies. It is another manifestation of Americans' unique exploitation of children as models for absolutist behavior standards and austere punishments that grown adults would not impose on themselves."[13]

Christian parents should not be duped by such histrionics. Scripture itself *prescribes* corporal discipline and cautions parents not to abandon the use of the rod. The opinions of self-proclaimed *experts* who disagree frankly amount to little. In the end, the facts will be found to agree with the Word of God. And in that vein, the *U.S. News* article actually offers some tidbits of very sound advice: "One lesson of the spanking controversy is that whether parents spank or not matters less than *how* they spank. . . . A single disapproving word can bring a sensitive child to tears, while a more spirited youngster might need stronger measures. Finally, spankings should be done in private to spare children humiliation and without anger."[14]

It might be worthwhile to reiterate a truth we stressed in chapter four. Parental discipline should never injure the child. It is never necessary to bruise your children in order to spank them hard enough to make your point. Spanking should always be administered with love and never when the *parent* is in a fit of rage. That sort of discipline is indeed abusive, wrong, and detrimental to the child, because it shatters the environment of loving nurture and instruction Ephesians 6:4 describes.

Furthermore, spanking is by no means the *only* kind of discipline parents should administer. There are many other viable forms of punishing children that, on occasion, can be used in addition to the rod. If the child responds immediately to a verbal rebuke in a given situation, a spanking is probably not necessary. Other punishments, such as withdrawing privileges, can also be used as occasional alternatives to spanking if the situation warrants it.

Much of our parental discipline should be totally positive. Parents can and should provide guidance for their children by rewarding them for positive behavior, as well as by punishing them for wrong behavior. Both sides of the equation are important. Positive motivation is entirely legitimate and can often be an effective means of getting children to obey. Notice, in fact, that the promise God Himself attached to the Fifth Commandment is a positive motivation. The commandment was reinforced with a promise, not a threat. It is often appropriate to say to your child, "If you do this, I will reward you in this way."

Balanced discipline involves both negative and positive reinforcements. In fact, we might sum up all discipline by saying it means *giving the appropriate reward for the conduct*. When the conduct (including both attitude and action) is good, a positive reward is warranted. When the conduct is bad, a negative reward is in order. It's not exactly rocket science, is it?

Yet parents seem incurably confused about these issues. Even many Christian parents I know are practically paralyzed with fear about whether, when, how, and how much to discipline their children. But what Scripture says is actually quite simple and straightforward: You have a depraved and foolish child, and if you want him not to be so foolish, spank him (Proverbs 22:15). You have a solemn responsibility before God to provide an environment of nurture and instruction where your child will constantly be exposed to God's truth (Deuteronomy 6:6–7). In short, you need to be careful not to provoke your children to wrath, but bring them up in the training and admonition of the Lord (Ephesians 6:4).

Any parent who masters those few, simple principles will not go far astray.

SEVEN

❧✗❧

The Father's Role

Husbands, love your wives.

—EPHESIANS 5:25

SEVEN

꒰ᆇ꒱

The Father's Role

Aside from the parents' fundamental commitment to Christ, the single most important foundation for successful parenting is a healthy, Christ-centered marriage.

I realize a statement like that may be discouraging to many readers, because so many today are struggling to be good parents in single-family homes, or in homes where at least one spouse has no commitment to Christ whatsoever.

If that describes your circumstances, don't despair. The situation is not hopeless as long as even *one* parent will undertake to raise the children in the nurture and admonition of the Lord. It is certainly difficult for one parent to work alone (and usually even *more* difficult when that lone parent must work *against* the ungodly example of the other parent), but it is certainly not hopeless in either case, because God Himself stands ready to fill the need.

He has not forgotten those single parents and children from broken homes. He is "a father of the fatherless [and] a defender of widows" (Psalm 68:5). In other words, He sustains the fatherless and widows with a special grace and lovingkindness. "The LORD watches over the strangers; He relieves the fatherless and widow" (Psalm 146:9). His very nature is to be a friend to the friendless and to meet the needs of the needy. Single parents can draw on His lovingkindness and take refuge in His immeasurable goodness.

But the single-parent home is clearly not God's ideal for the family. His design for families involves both father and mother. The father's role is so crucial that in Old Testament times, if a man died, his widow was to marry the next of kin (Deuteronomy 25:5). The archetypical family portrayed in Scripture involves both parents doing their part in submission to God, driven to work together by their mutual commitment to each other, with a deep, Christ-centered love as the glue that holds it all together. Therefore most of the teaching about family life in Scripture *assumes* the presence of two parents who are both committed to Christ. And in the biblical model, the marriage is therefore the focus and the foundation of the home.

Families these days tend to be child-centered instead. Everything revolves around the children. The children's activities, their relationships, and their interests tend to set the family agenda. But God's design for the family is that it be first Christ-centered, and then marriage-centered, with the husband-wife relationship taking priority over all other relationships in the home and the parents, not the children, determining the family agenda.

That is why in both places where the apostle Paul dealt with the family (Colossians 3:18–21 and Ephesians 5:22–6:4), he *began* his instructions with directions addressed to husbands and wives. In both places, the order he follows is the same:

- Wives, submit to your husbands (Colossians 3:18; Ephesians 5:22–24).

- Husbands, love your wives (Colossians 3:19; Ephesians 5:25–33).

- Children, obey your parents (Colossians 3:20; Ephesians 6:1–3).

- Parents, don't provoke your children to wrath (Colossians 3:21; Ephesians 6:4).

In both passages, the apostle also goes on to instruct servants to obey their masters, and the context suggests he had in mind primarily *household* servants (though the principle of submission would certainly apply to any kind of servant or employee). What Paul was doing in these two vital passages was setting forth God's design for how the family is to be ordered.

And the overriding theme of all of it is *submission*. There is to be a mutual submission among all parties, with the family as a whole submitting to the father's leadership; the father submitting himself in love to the fulfillment of the wife's essential needs; the children submitting themselves to the parents' authority; and even the parents submitting themselves to the children's needs by providing loving nurture and admonition without provoking them to wrath. Submission is the guiding principle all around: "Submitting yourselves one to another in the fear of God" (Ephesians 5:21).

In this study of parenting, we have followed the apostle's instructions, starting with children and moving backward. We first looked at the child's duty to obey. Then we examined the parents' duty to avoid exasperating their kids. Now we turn to the husband's role.

The apostle's instructions to husbands are simple: Love your wives. Love them as Christ loved the church. Cherish them. Honor them. Protect them. Serve them. Lead them. You are the head of the wife in the same sense that Christ is the head of the church.

THE MEANING OF LOVE

Ask many Christian husbands to summarize their biblical duty in one word, and they will answer, "leadership." Scripture answers the question with a different word: "love."

There is no doubt that God's design for husbands includes the aspect of leadership. But it is a leadership that flows from love and is always tempered by tender, caring affection. It is certainly true that the husband is the head of the wife. But as we shall see, "headship" in biblical terms means not merely authority. It does not even include the kind of authority many husbands want to assert over their families. It is not the fetch-me-my-slippers mentality many men convey to their wives and children. It is not a king-of-the-hill attitude. The husband is not to be a petty tyrant. His proper role as a loving, nurturing head is best epitomized by Christ, who took the servant's role to wash His disciples' feet.

Again, the theme that permeates Ephesians 5:22–6:4 is *submission,* and it is not without significance that the apostle's instructions to fathers come only two verses after the call for mutual submission. The New American Standard Bible renders verse 21 this way: "Be subject to one another in the fear of Christ." That's a general command to all Christians in all contexts.

Fathers are no exception to this rule. The love they are to show their wives involves submission. It is colored and characterized by meekness, tenderness, and service. It is a humble, servant's love like that of Christ.

Furthermore, to broaden the context a bit, the larger theme of this section of Ephesians 5 is about what it means to be *Spirit-filled.* Verse 18 says, "Do not be drunk with wine, in which is dissipation; but be filled with the Spirit." Why does the apostle connect the idea of drunkenness with the notion of being filled with the Spirit? The answer is not (as some would suggest) that being Spirit-filled is like being drunk. The truly Spirit-filled person is not someone who loses control of his faculties, acts erratically, dissolves into fits of laughter, or whatever. Unlike what many today think, Scripture never portrays Spirit-filled behavior as boisterous or out-of-control.

In fact, the whole idea of control is essential to the apostle's meaning here. A person filled with wine is literally *controlled* by wine. He is, as we say, "under the influence." Likewise, a person filled with the Spirit is under the control and influence of the Holy Spirit. His thoughts, actions, and treatment of others are all governed and shaped by the Holy Spirit's control.

What does Spirit-controlled behavior look like? Paul characterizes it this way: "Speaking to one another in psalms and hymns and spiritual songs, singing and making melody in your heart to the Lord, giving thanks always for all things to God the Father in the name of our Lord Jesus Christ, submitting to one another in the fear of God" (Ephesians 5:19–21). Notice the repetition of the words "one another." He starts with "speaking to one another" and ends with "submitting to one another." In between he describes a soul that is in harmony with the Lord and utterly thankful for every turn of Providence. He's describing someone whose heart and mind are so yielded to the Holy Spirit's control that from the mouth comes edifying speech, and from the heart comes a loving submission. In other words, the Spirit-filled individual is someone who *speaks* to edify, who *sings* praise to God from the depth of his heart, who *says* thanks to God for everything, and who *submits* to others in the fear of God.

Submission is what sets the stage for Paul's instructions to husbands: "Love your wives." The love he is calling for is a Spirit-filled, submissive love. This sort of love is frankly incompatible with the domineering, commanding way many husbands try to assert their rights as *head* of the family.

First Corinthians 13 contains the most thorough biblical description of love: "Love suffers long and is kind; love does not envy; love does not parade itself, is not puffed up; does not behave rudely, does not seek its own, is not provoked, thinks no evil; does not rejoice in iniquity, but rejoices in the truth; bears all things, believes all things, hopes all things, endures all things. Love never fails" (vv. 4–8).

Notice how the stress is on the utter selflessness of love—love's kindness, its gentleness, its refusal to be self-seeking, its utter concern for the welfare of its object. All those elements are essential aspects of what Paul calls for when he commands husbands to love their wives. Notice, also, that the apostle relies on verbs, not adjectives, to describe love. He begins and ends his description of love with *active* verbs ("suffers long . . . rejoices . . . bears . . . believes . . . hopes . . . endures"). Love is active, not passive, and the one who truly loves will show his love by what he does for the object of his love, not by demanding what he thinks should be done for him.

The husband who thinks God ordered the family so that his wife would be at his beck and call has it backward. *He* is to love and serve her. The father who thinks of his wife and children as personal possessions to be under his command has a skewed concept of the responsibility that is his as *head* of the family. His headship means first of all that he is to serve them, protect them, and provide for their needs. In short, his duty is *love*—and all that is encompassed in that word.

Wrapped up in the concept of headship are some crucial lessons about how love works.

THE MANNER OF LOVE

Notice, first of all, that the whole idea of the husband's headship is a comparison to Christ. The husband's headship over the wife is likened to Christ's headship over the church: "The husband is head of the wife, as also Christ is head of the church" (Ephesians 5:23). Therefore the husband's love for the wife is supposed to be like Christ's love for the church:

> Love your wives, *just as Christ also loved the church* and gave Himself for her, that He might sanctify and cleanse her with the washing of water by the word, that He might present her to Himself a glorious church, not having spot or wrinkle or any such thing, but that she should be holy and without blemish. So husbands ought to love their own wives as their own bodies; he who loves his wife loves himself. For no one ever hated his own flesh, but nourishes and cherishes it, just as the Lord does the church. For we are members of His body, of His flesh and of His bones. "For this reason a man shall leave his father and mother and be joined to his wife, and the two shall become one flesh." This is a great mystery, but I speak concerning Christ and the church. Nevertheless let each one of you in particular so love his own wife as himself, and let the wife see that she respects her husband. (Ephesians 5:25–33, emphasis added)

Surely it is significant that the apostle takes more time and gives more space to his instructions for husbands than for any other family member. This is no incidental part of his instructions for ordering the home life. It is a key, essential principle, and it is vital that husbands see the import of this passage: *Christ's love for the church is the pattern for the husband's love of the wife.* Paul highlights four aspects of this love.

It is a Sacrificial Love

First of all, as we have been stressing from the outset, the husband's love for his wife is not supposed to be a domineering kind of love. It is the love of self-sacrifice.

It is the same kind of love Christ had for the church. And how did He show His love? He "gave Himself for her" (Ephesians 5:25). Acts 20:28 refers to the church as "the church of God which He purchased with His own blood." The sacrifice of Christ is the very epitome of what love demands. First John 3:16 says, "By this we know love, because He laid down His life for us." Jesus Himself said, "Greater love has no one than this, than to lay down one's life for his friends" (John 15:13).

John Chrysostom, a great preacher in the early church, said this to husbands who might have been tempted to preoccupy themselves with defining the measure of obedience they expected from their wives:

> Hear also the measure of love. Wouldest thou have thy wife obedient unto thee, as the Church is to Christ? Take then thyself the same provident care for her as Christ takes for the Church. Yea, even if it shall be needful for thee to give thy life for her, yea, and to be cut into pieces ten thousand times, yea, and to endure and undergo any suffering whatever, refuse it not. Though thou shouldest undergo all this, yet wilt thou not, no, not even then, have done anything like Christ. For thou indeed art doing it for one to whom thou art already knit; but He for one who turned her back on Him and hated Him. In the same way then as He laid at His feet her who turned her back on Him, who hated, and spurned, and disdained Him, not by menaces, nor by violence, nor by terror, nor by anything else of the kind, but by his unwearied affection; so also do thou behave thyself toward thy wife. Yea, though thou see her looking down upon thee, and disdain-

166

ing, and scorning thee, yet by thy great thoughtfulness for her, by affection, by kindness, thou wilt be able to lay her at thy feet. . . . Yea, though thou shouldest suffer anything on her account, do not upbraid her; for neither did Christ do this.[1]

Although antiquated language, that's wonderful insight. How many men love to wave Ephesians 5:22—"Wives, submit to your own husbands"—in their wives' faces? Yet how many of those same men are willing to fulfill all that is demanded of *them* in verses 25–33?

Without actually using the word "love," the apostle Peter describes the husband's love for his wife: "Husbands, likewise, dwell with [your wives] with understanding, giving honor to the wife, as to the weaker vessel, and as being heirs together of the grace of life" (1 Peter 3:7).

Notice that Peter also affirms the submissive role of the wife. In verse 6, he says "Sarah obeyed Abraham, calling him lord." Not long ago a young man engaged to be married contacted a friend of mine for some biblical counsel. His engagement was in jeopardy, he said, because he had pointed out 1 Peter 3:6 to his future wife and instructed her that she should heretofore address him as "lord." (Actually, he said he preferred the New International Version, which says, "master.") She balked, telling him she didn't think the verse meant wives must literally address their husbands as "lord and master." This fellow contacted my friend for advice about whether he should break off the engagement now or give her time to learn "proper biblical submission."

My friend pointed out that 1 Peter 3:6 is not calling wives to a servile obeisance. A look at Genesis 18:12 reveals that when Sarah called Abraham "my lord," she was referring to him in the third person. Nothing suggests she *addressed* him that way, and there is certainly no biblical commandment that would require wives to address their husbands as superiors. For a husband to insist on that kind of verbal homage from his wife is to miss Peter's whole point. Peter's instructions to the *husband* in 1 Peter 3:7 stress that the wife is a fellow-heir of the grace of life—a spiritual equal before God, not the husband's personal minion.

My friend suggested to this fellow that perhaps he *should* break off the engagement, for the good of his future wife, until *he* gained a better perspective of how husbands are supposed to treat their wives.

The headship-submission relationship is not about superiority and inferiority. Many wives are frankly wiser, more knowledgeable, more articulate, and more discerning than their husbands. Yet God has ordered the family so that the man is the head. This is not because the wife automatically owes the husband servile deference as his inferior, for she is *not* to be treated as an inferior but as a joint heir. The reason for the divine order is because the wife is the *weaker* vessel, and the husband therefore owes her sacrifice and protection.

In other words, as far as husbands are concerned, the headship role should be seen as something that carries a greater responsibility, not greater privileges. At the heart of the biblical concept of headship is a willingness to sacrifice one's own privileges. A husband who cannot come to grips with that will not be exercising the proper kind of headship in his home.

I like to sum up the sacrificial nature of the husband's love with these three words:

Consideration. "Live with your wives in an understanding way," Peter says in verse seven (NASB). He's speaking of being considerate. This is opposite the cave-man mentality some today would advocate. It's incompatible with the kind of independent, proud, self-absorbed machismo many seem to think epitomizes true maleness. It calls for understanding, sensitivity, and meeting your wife's needs. It involves a sincere effort to understand her feelings, fears, anxieties, concerns, goals, dreams, and desires. In short, husbands must be considerate.

Often it boils down to listening. The husband must understand his wife's heart. How can he express a sacrificial love that meets her needs when he has no earthly idea what those needs are? This is frankly a struggle for most men. It is not something that comes naturally to us. Like our children, we wrestle against our own sinful tendencies and selfish desires. But God calls us to be models of sacrificial love in our families, and that begins by being considerate.

Chivalry. The wife is "the weaker vessel," according to Peter. In what sense are women *weaker?* This has reference primarily to the physical realm. Women are, as a class, physically weaker than men. Now, it is undoubtedly true that there are some men whose wives are physically more powerful than they are. But that is unusual, and I believe that even in the exceptional cases, the principle still applies. The man is to treat his wife with a gentle chivalry. He can do this in a thousand ways, from opening doors for her to moving furniture and doing the heavy work around the house.

A loving husband would not say to his wife, "After you've changed the tire I'll be glad to take you to the store." We serve them with our strength. We treat them as the weaker vessel, showing them a particular deference in those matters where their physical weakness places them at a disadvantage. First Peter 3:7 actually suggests that God *designed* women to be under the protection of a man, benefiting from his strength. And serving our wives by lending them that strength is one of the main ways we show them a Christlike, sacrificial love.

Communion. We're to regard our wives "as being heirs together of the grace of life." Men and women may be unequal physically, but they are equal spiritually. Treat your wife as a spiritual equal. While you're legitimately concerned with the task of spiritual leadership in your home, don't forget the responsibility of communion before God with your wife as joint heirs of His grace. Your role as her leader does not mean you are her superior. Both of you are utterly dependent on divine grace, and you are heirs together of that grace.

In the Song of Solomon, the wife says of her husband, "This is my beloved, and this is my friend" (5:16). I love that expression. She rejoices in her love for him, but it is not just his romantic devotion that thrills her. It is not his *machismo* or his leadership that causes her heart to sing. What is it? She is glad that he is her *friend.* That's the kind of relationship husbands should cultivate. It is a deep sense of intimate, equal sharing of spiritual things. It is a communion together like no other relationship on earth.

Here's a simple way of summarizing sacrificial love: The Spirit-filled husband loves his wife, not for what she can do for him, but because of what he can do for her. That is exactly how Christ's love works. He loves us not because there's something in us that attracts Him, not because He gains any benefit from loving us, but simply because He determined to love us and delights to bestow on us His favor.

Did you realize that love is an act of the will, not a feeling? Our generation tends to portray love as an involuntary feeling—a state into which people *fall.* Consequently, many who feel they have "fallen *out* of love" wrongly believe that there is nothing they can do about it, so they give up on their marriages. But here's proof that love is an act of the will: Scripture *commands* us to love. God is calling husbands to a deliberate, voluntary love, not a feeling they have no control over.

Love is not only a feeling. It is a commitment to the welfare of its object. It is a voluntary devotion. It involves sacrifice, consideration, chivalry, communion, courtesy, commitment, and all the other things we're talking about. *All of them are voluntary responses.* For a husband to protest that he *cannot* love his wife is sheer rebellion against the commandment of God.

It's not a question of deserving. Love is not something that must be *earned* by the lovableness of its object. We certainly did not do anything to earn Christ's love. He loved us in spite of our unattractiveness. His love for us is like the love of Hosea, whose wife defiled herself as a prostitute. And when her dissipation reached its lowest point, and she was put on a block to be auctioned off, Hosea himself bought her back (Hosea 3:1–3). He did this not because there was anything about her that was clean and sweet and gracious and lovely, but because it was in his heart to love her. God loved Israel the same way, despite her unfaithfulness. And Christ loves His church the same way, setting His affection on her and sacrificing Himself for her very life while she was yet in her sin. This is a love that is utterly and completely self-sacrificing.

Nor is Christ's love for us the kind of love that seeks to tyrannize us. It is a love that seeks to meet our needs, to understand us, and to provide strength for us. It is a sacrificial love. It is precisely the kind of love every husband owes his wife. And any man willing to obey God can, by the power of God's Spirit, muster that kind of love for his wife, regardless of what he may think is unlovable about her. This love is a fruit of God's Spirit. A love that serves and sacrifices is therefore the natural consequence of being Spirit-filled.

It is a Purifying Love

The love husbands are commanded to have for their wives is also a love that seeks and protects the purity of its object. "Christ loved the church and gave Himself for her, that He might sanctify and cleanse her with the washing of water by the word, that He might present her to Himself a glorious church, not having spot or wrinkle or any such thing, but that she should be holy and without blemish" (Ephesians 5:25–27).

Now this makes a beautiful picture. It suggests that Christ's love for the church is something that drives Him to make her pure and keep her pure. He wants to clothe the church in glory. The Greek word translated "glorious" in verse 27 is *endoxos*, which speaks of a gorgeous splendor. Luke 7:25 uses the same word, and the English version translates it "gorgeously appareled."

It speaks of a pure, spotless beauty that He communicates to her. It is Christ's own glory bestowed on the church. It is the splendor of His holiness and virtue—without stain, without wrinkle, and without flaw.

When a man truly loves his wife, her purity should be his supreme concern. No one would ever want to defile a person whom he really loves. The young man who says he loves his fiancée but wants her to have sex with him before marriage is not driven by love at all. That's sheer lust. Love honors and protects the purity of its object.

Husband, if you really love your wife, you'll hate anything that defiles her. Whatever threatens to steal her purity will become to you a mortal enemy. And conversely, any so-called "love" that drags a partner through uncleanness is a false love.

I'm amazed at how many men I hear about who deliberately expose their wives to salacious films, magazines, or lewd and indecent images, thinking it's a justifiable way to put some spark back into their romantic relationship. I once heard a preacher (a man who claimed to be an evangelical) on a television talk show boasting that his wife bought him a subscription to *Playboy*, and they read the magazines together. "When you're our age," he said with a smarmy smugness, "you need something to put the spark back in your romance." That man was a disgrace to the name of Christ, and he dishonored his own wife as much as he dishonored the Lord. I cannot envision a man who loves his wife wanting her to be exposed to any kind of wickedness and filth, not to mention subjecting himself to unnecessary temptation, for any reason whatsoever. That sort of activity will certainly offer no long-term help to a failing romance. All it does is defile and besmirch both parties.

Husbands should never lead their wives into any kind of sin. There is never any good reason to expose her to iniquity. Don't draw her into anything that might tempt her, dishonor her, or debase her. Don't drag her to see movies where her ears will be assaulted with gratuitous profanity. Don't take her to any form of entertainment that might appeal to sinful lusts. Don't irritate her or embitter her so that she falls to the temptation of anger. Don't tempt her in any way. And be an example of purity yourself.

Above all, if you do nothing else in the life of your spouse, expose her to the Word of God. Keep her under the hearing of the Word of God so that she might be daily, routinely cleansed. You serve in a priestly role as head of your home, and a vital part of your priestly task is to help guard your wife's purity.

Occasionally husbands will come to me and say things like, "I don't know what went wrong, but all of a sudden my wife left me for another man." The sad truth is that when a woman sins like that, it is never the beginning of something going wrong; it's inevitably the *end* of something that went wrong long ago. When a woman leaves her husband, it is almost certainly the culmination of a long pattern of sin. Had that husband been diligently guarding his wife's purity, as was his responsibility, he probably would never have been caught off guard in such a way, and he may have been able to do something to keep her from falling.

The urgency of protecting our wives' purity is amplified in a culture where millions of men daily send their wives into a worldly workforce, to work under someone else's supervision, shoulder to shoulder with some very powerful temptations. The wife spends her day in an office environment with other well-dressed, successful men. She is dressed for the business environment as well. Everything out there looks pretty good compared to what she encounters at home. I know from the testimonies of people whom I have counseled that this kind of thing has been the starting point for the dissolution of many marriages.

Husbands need to be alert to these dangers and avoid them. Husbands also must keep themselves pure in the workplace. The man who flirts with his secretary or other women is not honoring his wife, and he is jeopardizing her purity as well, because anything that defiles him will ultimately defile her.

First Corinthians 13:6 says love "does not rejoice in iniquity, but rejoices in the truth." Real love could never find pleasure in iniquity, especially the kind of iniquity that defiles the object of love. Genuine love is concerned for purity. And the husband who truly loves his wife deems it a privilege, an honor, and a joy to guard her purity. What a benediction and blessing a pure wife brings on his life!

It is a Caring Love

"Husbands ought to love their own wives as their own bodies; he who loves his wife loves himself. For no one ever hated his own flesh, but nourishes and cherishes it, just as the Lord does the church. For we are members of His body, of His flesh and of His bones" (Ephesians 5:28–30).

What does it mean to love your wife as your own body? It's actually quite a simple concept. You take care of your own body. If it's sick, you put it in bed so it can get better. If it's hungry, you feed it. If it's thirsty, you give it something to drink. If it's disheveled, you clean it. You take care of it constantly—feeding, clothing, comforting, and providing whatever it needs. And that's the very essence of the love you ought to show your wife. You are to be preoccupied with meeting her needs.

The comparison with caring for one's body is especially apropos in marriage, because of the way God established marriage to be. Paul goes on to quote from Genesis, where God first established marriage as an institution: "Therefore a man shall leave his father and mother and be joined to his wife, and they shall become one flesh" (Genesis 2:24; Ephesians 5:31).

When a man and woman get married they become one. And the marriage union is consummated with the literal bodily union of husband and wife. The two become one flesh. From that point on, the husband should consider that, if his wife's needs are not being met, his needs are not being met, either. He is to give her the same care and consideration he gives his own body.

We have a little sign that hangs in the kitchen at our home: "If mamma ain't happy, ain't nobody happy." The principle is certainly true in marriage. The husband who allows his wife's needs to go unmet will soon feel the pain of it! And rightfully so. If you want to be a fulfilled husband, you must have a fulfilled wife. If you want happiness and harmony in your marriage, then treat your wife as well as you treat yourself. If you want to be a fulfilled father, you must have fulfilled children.

The apostle Paul says, "No one ever hated his own flesh." It is simply not normal to hate yourself. Even people who claim to have a low self-image are usually actually expressing a kind of self-centered pride, not true self-loathing. After all, they avoid things that hurt them; they eat when they are hungry; they have the same self-preservation instincts as anyone else. They don't really *hate* themselves. In fact, most people who think they have low self-esteem actually pamper themselves more than the average person.

It's normal to take care of one's own needs. There's nothing wrong with it, unless we fail to show similar consideration to others (Mark 12:31). Certainly the normal attitude of a husband toward his wife ought to include a loving care for her. Something is seriously wrong and unhealthy if the husband doesn't nourish and cherish his wife the way he would his own body. A husband's perspective is horribly twisted if he thinks of his wife as his personal cook, laundry maid, babysitter, and sex partner, and nothing more. It is particularly unconscionable if he puts her in the place of the breadwinner. She is a God-given treasure to be cared for, to be cherished, to be nourished, to be a loving helper, to fulfill her husband's need for love, for companionship, for physical intimacy, for partnership, and for friendship, and to be the mother of his children. Husband and wife are one flesh. It is the most perfect union on earth. And the husband who truly understands his union with his wife will naturally care for her the same way he cares for himself.

This principle has an even deeper significance in a Christian marriage. The wife is not only one with the husband; she is one with Christ as well. In her marriage she is one with the husband; in her salvation she is one with Christ. So how the husband treats her reflects how he regards the Lord. Jesus Himself said this: "Inasmuch as you did it to one of the least of these My brethren, you did it to Me" (Matthew 25:40). Certainly that principle applies more than ever in a Christian marriage.

The apostle underscores all this with two words in Ephesians 5:29: *ektrephō* (nourishes) and *thalpō* (cherishes).

Ektrephō is used only one other place in the New Testament, Ephesians 6:4 (a verse already familiar to us), where it is translated, "Bring them up." Husbands are called to nurture and feed their wives and bring them to maturity in a way similar to how parents nourish and care for their children. This suggests that he is to provide for her needs, feed her (both spiritually and literally), and help bring her to spiritual maturity. This not only underscores the man's responsibility to be the breadwinner, but it also highlights his responsibility to take the role of spiritual leadership in the family.

Thalpō literally means "to warm with body heat." It's a beautiful expression, emphasizing the intimacy and tenderness of the husband's duty to the wife. The Greek word was sometimes used to describe a nesting bird, and it is so used in 1 Thessalonians 2:7. It evokes the image of providing a nest, giving warmth and security, and tenderly cherishing her as something fragile and precious.

Our society has it backward. Women are pressured to be tough and independent, and men are made to be weak and effeminate. Women are encouraged to leave the home and strive for success in the business world, and men are chided for being too protective. Many women actually resent the idea that husbands should nourish and cherish their wives, but this is a clear biblical command. It is how God has ordered the family. The wife is not called to be the nourisher. She is not assigned the role of provider. That is the husband's responsibility. And if a man doesn't provide for his family, according to 1 Timothy 5:8, "he has denied the faith and is worse than an unbeliever."

Husbands and fathers, we are the providers and the protectors for our wives and our children. When their needs are met, and we care for them as we would care for ourselves, then we are showing the kind of caring love God wants us to bestow on our families.

It is an Enduring Love

The husband's love must also be an unbreakable love. It is to persevere despite all trials and obstacles. God Himself has designed marriage this way: "For this reason a man shall leave his father and mother and be joined to his wife, and the two shall become one flesh" (Ephesians 5:31). Christ emphasized the permanence of this union: "So then, they are no longer two but one flesh. Therefore what God has joined together, let not man separate" (Matthew 19:6).

The marriage union is fundamentally a *physical* union: "The two shall become one flesh." This refers, of course to the sexual union between husband and wife. And the fruits of that union, their children, bear the genetic pattern of two people having become one flesh. It is one of the most amazing wonders of God's creation. It starts with the physical union of husband and wife. The life of the man is joined with the life of the woman, and in the intimacy of that physical relationship, the two become one flesh. This is such a sacred union that the apostle Paul warned the Corinthians of the dangers of corrupting it promiscuously: "Or do you not know that he who is joined to a harlot is one body with her" (1 Corinthians 6:16)? To violate the marriage in such a way not only defiles the union between husband and wife; it also defiles the union between Christ and Christian. "Shall I then take the members of Christ and make them members of a harlot? Certainly not" (v. 15)!

But beyond the physical union of husband and wife is also a *spiritual* union. *God* joins them together (Matthew 19:6). The marriage union engulfs every aspect of life—emotions, intellect, body, personality, likes and dislikes, worship, service, private life, and public life. All such things are shared by husband and wife. The two become one in an inexplicably intimate way. That is God's design for marriage.

In a sense, even individual identity is lost when the two become one. They are like a new person, co-mingled with a life partner, clinging to one another, sharing with one another, inextricably united by God Himself. That is why "the Lord God of Israel says that He hates divorce" (Malachi 2:16).

Now look again at what Paul is saying about marriage in Ephesians 5:31: "A man shall leave his father and mother and be joined to his wife." In the familiar King James Version of Genesis 2:24, the key words are "leave" and "cleave."

Leaving. The Greek word translated "leave" in Ephesians 5:31 is *kataleipō,* an intensified verb meaning "to leave behind" or "to abandon completely." There's a vital severing of the parent-child relationship that must occur when a couple gets married. Marriage doesn't utterly terminate the relationship with parents, of course. Nor does it eliminate the child's responsibility to honor the father and mother. But it does take the child out from under the parents' direct chain of command, and it establishes a whole new home with a whole new headship. The new husband becomes head of the wife. The married couple are no longer children under their parents' direct oversight, and the parents are no longer directly responsible for them. Leaving father and mother is an essential part of every marriage. When young couples try to "cleave" but have forgotten to "leave," it creates havoc in the young marriage.

Cleaving. The word translated "be joined to" is *proskollaō,* which literally means "to be glued to." The initial oneness of physical union incorporates a oneness of mind, a oneness of purpose, a oneness of heart, and a oneness of emotion. Having left their parents, breaking an incredibly secure bond, they now join together to form a new union that in the plan of God is supposed to be unbreakable.

THE MOTIVE OF LOVE

The *meaning* of love is summed up in the word "submission." The *manner* of love is "sacrifice"—defined by Christ's self-giving love for His church. What is the *motive* of the husband's love for his wife?

"This is a great mystery," Paul writes, "but I speak concerning Christ and the church. Nevertheless let each one of you in particular so love his own wife as himself, and let the wife see that she respects her husband" (Ephesians 5:32–33). Here is the motive: love's *sacredness.*

Marriage is a picture of Christ and the church. It is a sacred mystery. In fact, the sacredness of Christ's church is linked to the sacredness of marriage. Christ is the heavenly Bridegroom and the church is His bride (Revelation 21:9). Marriage illustrates this union. The husband is called to be Christlike in his love for his wife because this protects the sacredness of the divine object lesson. The Christian husband therefore displays what he thinks of Christ by the way he treats his wife. And marriage itself is a sacred institution because of what it illustrates.

That's the best motive I know for a husband to love his wife. His love for her honors Christ. How he treats her is a testimony not only to the wife, but also to the world at large about Christ's love for His people. The husband who understands this sacred mystery will delight to love, purify, protect, and care for his wife. And this sacred union is the foundation from which fathers nourish and encourage their children toward maturity.

EIGHT

The Mother's Role

Wives, submit yourselves unto your own husbands,
as unto the Lord

—EPHESIANS 5:22

EIGHT

The Mother's Role

As early as the fourth chapter of Genesis, the family—the first divinely ordained institution—is under attack. The first child born, Cain, grew up to kill his younger brother Abel. And by the end of the Book of Genesis, the chronicle of early humanity reads like a Who's Who of dysfunctional families.

Not only was that first family torn by sibling rivalry, but in the generations that followed, virtually all their offspring also descended into further sin with alarming speed. Cain's family line is traced in the second half of Genesis four. There we meet Lamech, evidently the first polygamist, who killed someone and wrote a boasting poem about it for one of his wives. Adam's family line is traced further in Genesis five. There we first encounter Noah, patriarch of the one family God preserved when He destroyed the whole world because of humanity's unrelenting pursuit of evil.

But even Noah's family is no model of family values. Genesis nine recounts how Noah became drunk. While he was in a catatonic stupor, one of his sons, Ham, uncovered Noah's nakedness and boasted about it to his brothers. Noah's response was to curse Ham and all his progeny. Noah's own offspring did not fare particularly well, either. All the nations they produced soon adopted all the trappings of paganism. Polygamy, lust, adultery, incest, and a host of other abominations continued to dominate the human family. In fact, the same sins that had corrupted humanity before the Flood continued unabated afterward. (Compare Genesis 6:5 with 8:21.) Before long, God judged the world again, this time by confounding the languages at Babel.

Then God called Abraham. He is the paragon of faith, but his family life is no model. He and his wife Sarah contrived to produce offspring through an illicit sexual union between Abraham and Sarah's handmaid, Hagar. The son produced by that union was Ishmael, who vied with his half-brother Isaac for Abraham's affections and tore the family apart. Isaac's twin sons, Esau and Jacob, became bitter rivals, splitting that generation of the family, too. In the next generation, Jacob's elder sons sold their younger brother Joseph into slavery and lied to their father about it. Without exception, every generation in Genesis had its share of family problems. But God is faithful. Through one troubled generation after another, He nonetheless kept the line of Messianic promise alive, not because of how the families were, but in spite of it.

The beginning and the end of Genesis make an interesting contrast. The book starts with the words "In the beginning God . . . " (1:1) but ends with the words " . . . in a coffin in Egypt" (50:26). The opening chapter of Genesis is all about creation; the closing chapter is all about death. At the beginning, Adam is placed in a beautiful garden surrounded by life and divine blessings. At the end, the body of Jacob is interred in a cave with the bodies of Abraham, Sarah, Isaac, Rebekah, and Leah. And the family in which the messianic bloodline resided was in exile in Egypt.

Genesis is all about how sin destroys what God created to be good. And one of the themes that stands out most clearly as we read about the decline of humanity in Genesis is the horrible toll of sin on the institution of the family. From the time Adam sinned and tainted the whole race with corruption until this present day, families have struggled.

As a matter of fact, family problems are inherent in the curse of Adam's sin. God addressed this aspect of the curse to Eve: "To the woman He said: 'I will greatly multiply your sorrow and your conception; in pain you shall bring forth children; *your desire shall be for your husband, and he shall rule over you*'" (Genesis 3:16, emphasis added). In addition to the increased pain of childbirth, the woman would have to bear the frustration of a perpetual struggle between herself and her husband in the marriage relationship. Compare the above highlighted phrase from Genesis 3:16 with a similar expression in Genesis 4:7, which uses identical words and identical grammar in both English and Hebrew: "Sin lies at the door. And *its desire is for you, but you should rule over it*" (emphasis added).

The "desire" spoken of in Genesis 3:16 is not the woman's sexual or emotional desire for her husband. It is an illicit desire to usurp his headship. It is exactly like sin's desire to master us, described in precisely the same words in 4:7. The Hebrew word translated "desire" in both verses is *teshuqah,* which comes from an Arabic root that means "to compel; to seek control over."

Furthermore, the word for "rule" in both 3:16 and 4:7 is a different word from the Hebrew words used in Genesis 1:28 where God first commanded Adam to "subdue" the earth and "have dominion" over it. Adam was given a legitimate dominion over his wife; but under sin he would corrupt that dominion into a totally different, despotic, sort of rule. Compare the two passages again. In Genesis 4:7 God was warning Cain that sin wanted to gain control over him, but he should gain the mastery over sin instead. Using a parallel expression in Genesis 3:16, the Lord was warning Eve that one of the bitter consequences of her sin would be a perpetual struggle with her husband. She would attempt to usurp his authority. And he would respond by trying to impose a despotic, authoritarian rule over her that would suppress her in a way God never intended.

We see those very consequences at work in the failure of millions of families to this present day. Women try to take charge and overturn the divine order in the home; and men respond with a domineering, tyrannical authority God never granted them.

In other words, conflicts between husbands and wives are a fruit of humanity's fallenness. This is true in precisely the same way a child's misbehavior is a display of the child's depravity. You might ask, "What chance does a marriage have?" And the answer is "slim," especially for people without Christ.

The institution of marriage faces a particular danger today with the rise of the feminist movement. Many radical feminists have openly called for the end of marriage as an institution. For example, a document that helped shaped the modern feminist agenda was called "A Declaration of Feminism." It included this statement: "Marriage has existed for the benefit of men and has been a legally sanctioned method of control over women. The end of the institution of marriage is a necessary condition for the liberation of woman. Therefore it is important for us to encourage women to leave their husbands and not to live individually with men. Now we know that it is the institution of marriage that has failed us, and we must work to destroy it."

Most feminists are more subtle than that, of course. Rather than calling for an end to marriage *per se,* they simply deny the wife's duty to submit to her husband. Driven by the same desire to usurp their husbands' authority that was inherent in the Genesis 3:16 curse, they will not be satisfied with the *spiritual* equality Scripture says exists between husband and wife. They are determined to eradicate authority and submission in marriage altogether. While such a goal may sound merely egalitarian and equitable, it is actually a recipe for chaos at the most basic level. It undermines the cohesiveness of the family unit by establishing an anarchy, with no one in charge and everyone simply doing what is right in his own eyes. Overturning the biblical lines of authority in a family doesn't eliminate conflicts; it multiplies them.

As we observed in the previous chapter, there is a true sense in which husbands and wives—and all believers, for that matter—are to submit themselves to one another (Ephesians 5:21). There is also a spiritual equality between husbands and wives in marriage. They are "heirs together of the grace of life" (1 Peter 3:7). In the Body of Christ, "There is neither Jew nor Greek, there is neither slave nor free, there is neither male nor female; for you are all one" (Galatians 3:28). So there is a kind of equality that places husband and wife on an equal footing before God.

But this spiritual equality does not eliminate the need for an authority structure in the family. So Scripture makes the arrangement unmistakable: "Wives, submit to your own husbands, as to the Lord. For the husband is head of the wife, as also Christ is head of the church" (Ephesians 5:22–23).

The husband is thus given authority in the marriage, and the wife is commanded to follow his leadership. In a similar way, parents are given authority in the family, and the children are told to follow. There *is* a true spiritual equality among all parties. The wife may be intellectually equal to or wiser than her husband. The children may also have gifts and talents that are equal or superior to the parents'. But those kinds of equality do not nullify the important God-ordained differences between the roles. Scripture is inescapably clear on this: A certain authority, matched by a corresponding responsibility, is intrinsic to the husband's proper role. And the wife is to submit to that authority.

As we saw in the previous chapter, the husband's responsibility includes the duty to provide, protect, shelter, nourish, and cherish his family, and his wife in particular. Along with that responsibility comes an authority to which the wife is commanded to submit. The extra measure of responsibility and the extra measure of authority are inextricably linked. The husband must shoulder the responsibility of providing for the family, and along with that responsibility comes the authority to make decisions about the management of family finances. If it is his duty to protect his family and provide a place for them to live, he must also be given authority in all decisions related to these issues.

There is nothing to prohibit a man from seeking his wife's counsel about matters such as where the family should live, what job offer he should accept, whether the family should participate in this or that activity, or a host of other similar decisions. In fact, the man who is *not* interested in his wife's opinion in such matters is a foolish and uncaring husband. But final decisions are ultimately the husband's prerogative, because he is the one who will be accountable to God for the stewardship of his family.

The wife is commanded to submit. This is so basic to the wife's duties that the apostle Paul underscores it as one of the fundamental lessons older women in the church are to teach younger women: "Admonish the young women to love their husbands, to love their children, to be discreet, chaste, homemakers, good, obedient to their own husbands, that the word of God may not be blasphemed" (Titus 2:4–5).

Colossians 3:18 echoes the same idea: "Wives, submit to your own husbands, as is fitting in the Lord." There the apostle makes clear that this is not a cultural preference; it is a commandment from God himself. The wife's submission is *"fitting* in the Lord." The Greek word translated "fitting" is *aneko,* which speaks of something that is proper, apropos. Paul uses the word only two other places in his epistles. One is Ephesians 5:4, where he says filthy talk and coarse jesting among saints "are not fitting" (*aneko*). The other is in Philemon eight, where he tells Philemon "to command . . . what is fitting" (*aneko*). In each case, he employs the term either to enjoin obedience to what is "fitting," or to forbid the practice of what is "not fitting." In Pauline terms, then, to say something is "fitting" (*aneko*) is tantamount to declaring it a binding principle of God's moral law.

The wife's duty to submit to her husband is, therefore, not optional. The wife's submission is a mandatory aspect of her role as wife and mother. And to violate or abandon that principle is to undermine the very foundation of her own family. Proverbs 14:1 says, "The wise woman builds her house, but the foolish pulls it down with her hands." And one of the surest ways to tear down a household is to abandon the authority structure God has established for the family.

Now we must confront this subject candidly: Even many Christians are baffled about how the authority-submission balance is supposed to work in the marriage. Are there no limits on the wife's duty to submit? What if the husband is a non-Christian? Does this command to submit make the woman a second-class citizen? Does it mean all women are supposed to submit to all men as a class?

Let's delve a little more deeply into this subject by dealing with some of the most fundamental questions about the wife's submission.

TO WHOM DOES SHE SUBMIT?

First, to whom does a woman submit? Is every woman supposed to submit to every man? Are women as a class under the authority of men?

Scripture is very clear about this: "Wives, submit *to your own husbands*. . . . Just as the church is subject to Christ, so let the wives be *to their own husbands*" (Ephesians 5:22, 24, emphasis added). The same phrase is repeated in virtually every verse that commands wives to obey: "Wives, submit *to your own husbands*" (Colossians 3:18). Older women should teach younger women to be "obedient *to their own husbands*" (Titus 2:5). "Wives, likewise, be submissive *to your own husbands*. . . . For in this manner, in former times, the holy women who trusted in God also adorned themselves, being submissive *to their own husbands*" (1 Peter 3:1, 5 emphasis added in all the preceding quotations).

Again and again, Scripture stresses the principle: Wives are to submit *to their own husbands.* My wife has no duty to submit to any other man merely on the grounds that he is a man and she is a woman. If a man believes his maleness gives him inherent authority over all women as a class, he misunderstands Scripture.

In fact, the one institution outside marriage where God expressly limits the hierarchy to male leadership is the church. Men, not women, are to have the teaching and administrative authority in the church. Paul says, "Let a woman learn in silence with all submission. And I do not permit a woman to teach or to have authority over a man, but to be in silence" (1 Timothy 2:11–12). The context of that verse shows that it refers to leadership roles in the church. Paul is saying that in the church, women are not to take teaching assignments that involve teaching men, nor are they permitted to hold positions of administrative authority over men. He continues with the theme of church leadership in the verses that immediately follow, giving the requirements for office-holders in the church. In outlining those guidelines, he makes it clear that elders and deacons must be faithful *men* (1 Timothy 3:1–13). Then in 1 Corinthians 14:34–35, he writes, "Let your women keep silent in the churches, for they are not permitted to speak; but they are to be submissive, as the law also says. And if they want to learn something, let them ask their own husbands at home; for it is shameful for women to speak in church." Everywhere Scripture speaks about leadership roles in the church, it portrays church leadership as a man's role.

Nothing in Scripture ever suggests, however, that every woman must submit to every man in every situation. In the context of the church, women are called to submit to the men under whose oversight God has placed the church. But notice that other men in the church are *also* commanded to submit to the shepherds of the flock (Hebrews 13:17). Nowhere does Scripture command the woman to treat every man in the church as if he were in authority over her. And nowhere does Scripture give men as a class any authority over women who are not their wives. A woman is required to submit only to those men with legitimate authority over her. In the context of the church, that would be the elders. In the context of marriage and family life, that is *"her own husband."*

Remember, the husband's responsibility to nurture and care for his wife is what justifies his authority over her. Men with no such responsibility for a woman's welfare have no right to pretend authority over her merely by virtue of the fact that they are male.

Even the elders of a church have no authority to intrude into the family and wield authority over a woman in the context of her home and family life (unless she is involved in some clear-cut violation of Scripture that requires the kind of discipline prescribed in Matthew 18). Elders have no intrinsic authority to make personal decisions for church members and no right to command them regarding extrabiblical issues in their private lives. Their authority covers church ministry and the teaching and enforcing of the Word of God. They have no jurisdiction over flock members' private matters. In fact, notice that Paul says if women have questions about the teaching in the church, "let them ask their own husbands at home" (1 Corinthians 14:35). So even the task of answering a woman's spiritual questions is first of all *her own husband's* duty, not the automatic prerogative of her church's elders.

One of the great disadvantages for a wife who is in the workforce full time is this: She is often forced to submit to men other than her own husband. God's prescribed order is overturned. Clashes between the woman's authority figure at work and her husband in the home are inevitable. Many bosses have no compunctions about ordering a woman in the workplace to sacrifice her priorities in the home. This is especially true if the woman's professional career involves travel. She is taken out of the home, removed from her own husband's care and authority, and placed under a totally different chain of command. It therefore becomes practically impossible for most career women to fulfill the command to be "keepers at home" (Titus 2:5, KJV).

Mothers in particular pay a high price when they leave the home to pursue a career. Not only do they step out of the role God has designed for wives, but they often must also abandon their most crucial role as the primary caregiver to their own children. I believe one of the worst errors a mother can make is to sacrifice time with her own children for the sake of pursuing a career.

I realize these are not popular or politically correct opinions as we enter the twenty-first century. But I am constrained to teach what the Word of God says. Scripture portrays the ideal woman as a keeper of the home who is subject to her own husband, not a career woman whose family takes second place.

The independent working wife has become the primary symbol of woman's rebellion against God's order. More than 50 percent of all women are now in the work force. The numbers now exceed fifty million working mothers. And most of them have school-aged children (or younger). Two of every three children aged three to five years old now spend part of their day in facilities outside the home. Their mothers have abdicated the maternal role in favor of a career or personal fulfillment.

The United States government now offers tax credits for child care, just so that mothers can go to work. The results on our nation's marriages and families have been absolutely devastating. These mothers, in effect, have abandoned the home. They have removed themselves from the oversight of "their own husbands," and they are fighting for their independence in the workplace. In the process, many have literally abandoned home, children, and husband in every sense, opting for divorce when career and family conflicts become too much.

I would also identify the working-mother syndrome as one of the most important reasons so many modern parents are at a loss to know how to raise their children. Having abandoned something as fundamental as God's order for the home, how can they hope to find *any* parenting methodology that will be effective?

When a mother relinquishes God's order, the whole family feels the result. God's design for the woman is to be in the home—to be submissive to her own husband, to be caring for her own children, and to be tending the needs of her own home. Mothers who want to be successful parents cannot forsake those tasks and expect the Lord's blessing in their parenting. Being a mother is not a part-time task. It cannot be treated as a sideline. The mom, even more than the dad, must be devoted to parenting full-time. The home is her domain.

Some protest that this makes the woman a second-class citizen, removed from the workforce, cut off from any influence, unable to make her mark in the world. But Scripture says the opposite. A woman's greatest influence is manifest through her children. She is the one who influences them more than any other, including the father, because of her constant presence in the home. She is rescued from any second-class status by this lofty role.

I believe that is precisely what the apostle Paul meant in 1 Timothy 2:13-15: "For Adam was formed first, then Eve. And Adam was not deceived, but the woman being deceived, fell into transgression. Nevertheless she will be saved in childbearing if they continue in faith, love, and holiness, with self-control." In other words, the man was created first, but the woman fell into sin first. Her only primacy was a disgrace. Now because of the curse, she tends to be relegated to a role of subservience under a tyrannical kind of leadership. Nonetheless, she recovers herself from the ignominy of this situation, and from the stigma of having led the race into sin, by her role and her influence as a mother who leads her children into righteousness.

To be a mother is by no means second class. Men may have the *authority* in the home, but the women have the *influence.* The mother, more than the father, is the one who molds and shapes those little lives from day one. She takes them into her own heart and nurses them from the earliest moments of their lives. As they grow, she is the one who is there more of the time, binding up their little wounds and taking them through the issues of life, day in and day out. And the father usually shows up after work to pontificate and issue orders. Oh, he can play with the kids and teach them things and discipline them when they need it and even win their affection in the process. But he will rarely have the same place in their hearts as Mom. Ever watch a big, strapping linebacker on the sidelines when he knows he is in the camera's eye? Inevitably he will wave and say, "Hi, Mom!" I have seen it a thousand times—but

I have *never* seen one say, "Hi, Dad!" I know coaches who tell me they never recruit athletes; they recruit their mothers. If the mother likes you, you're in. No one else, not even the father, has that kind of influence.

Mothers, don't let anyone ever dupe you into thinking there's anything ignoble or disgraceful about remaining at home and raising your family. Don't buy the lie that you're repressed if you're a worker in the home instead of in the world's workplace. Devoting yourself fully to your role as wife and mother is not repression; it is true liberation. Multitudes of women have bought the world's lie, put on a suit, picked up a briefcase, dropped their children off for someone else to raise, and gone into the workplace, only to realize after fifteen years that they and their children have a hollow void in their hearts. Many such career women now say they wish they had devoted themselves to motherhood and the home instead.

"Keeper at home" is the role God designed for wives to fill (Titus 2:5; Proverbs 31). He has instructed wives and mothers to submit to their own husbands, rather than place themselves under the domination of others outside the home. It is there, under her own husband's authority, that the truly godly woman flourishes. That is where she finds her greatest joy. And that is where she has her greatest influence.

WHY DOES SHE SUBMIT?

Why must wives submit to their husbands? "For the husband is head of the wife, as also Christ is head of the church; and He is the Savior of the body" (Ephesians 5:23). As we saw in the preceding chapter, marriage is a picture, an object lesson, about Christ and the church. Just as Christ is the head of the church, so the husband is the head of the wife.

The order in a marriage is therefore a sacred emblem. A woman who refuses to submit to her husband corrupts the meaning of the divine institution.

Furthermore, the woman's submission to her husband is established in the order of creation; it is the natural and proper order of things. The apostle Paul, calling for women to display submissive attitudes in public worship, wrote, "For man is not from woman, but woman from man. Nor was man created for the woman, but woman for the man" (1 Corinthians 14:8-9). He employs a similar argument in 1 Timothy 2:13: "For Adam was formed first, then Eve." Here is the point: Eve was created to be a helper to Adam—to keep him company, to support and encourage him, to work alongside him. She was created for the express purpose of being his wife and helpmate, not to pursue an agenda independently of him.

And to this day, the woman's role in the marriage relationship is designed to fulfill those same purposes. Why? Because Eve was God's gracious gift to Adam. Her role as his wife was a token of the marvelous grace of God to man. And even now, a woman's submission to her husband is a wonderful expression of divine grace. If she abandons that role, it is like stealing God's grace from her family.

But God has designed men and women to find their greatest fulfillment through obedience to the roles He has sovereignly appointed them. In other words, God's order in the home reflects His *gracious* purposes, not some sinister design to put women down.

HOW DOES SHE SUBMIT?

How does the wife submit? "Therefore, just as the church is subject to Christ, so let the wives be to their own husbands in everything" (Ephesians 5:24). That sets a very high standard for the wife's submission. She is to submit to her husband like the church submits to Christ.

How does the church submit to Christ? With love for Him as the primary motive behind all obedience. This verse is not putting the husband in the role of God and making wives into abject slaves. The wife is not the husband's lackey, any more than the church is supposed to cower and grovel before Christ. Rather, what this calls for is a willing, agreeable heart. It certainly rules out proud rebellion and haughty defiance. But it also means that the wife should not render her compliance grudgingly or with an embittered spirit. She should follow her husband because of her deep love for him, just as the church follows Christ out of love for him.

Furthermore, she should obey because he is her head, just as Christ is the head of the church. The head gives direction, and the body naturally responds. When a physical body does not respond correctly to its own head, the result is either an incapacitating paralysis or uncontrolled seizures. Either way, it is debilitating to the body. Likewise, a wife who will not respond to the direction of her head impairs her own ability to function correctly.

But submission doesn't mean the wife must lose her own personality. It doesn't mean she becomes a robot. It doesn't mean she has to become bland and lifeless and monotonous. It doesn't mean she should always stifle her own opinion. But it means that deep down in her heart there should be "a gentle and quiet spirit, which is very precious in the sight of God" (1 Peter 3:4). The wife who willingly and lovingly responds to her husband's leadership with such a spirit honors her Lord, her husband, her children, her church, and herself.

HOW FAR DOES SHE SUBMIT?

Finally, how far does the wife need to submit? "As the church is subject to Christ, so let the wives be to their own husbands *in everything*" (Ephesians 5:24, emphasis added). Authority in the home is not parceled out between husband and wife. Family issues aren't partitioned into categories and divided up, so that the husband has authority in the area of finances, but the wife makes decisions pertaining to the children. The wife *does* have a certain authority over the children, of course, but ultimately even in that she is to be subject to her husband. Final authority is assigned by God to him. He is certainly free to consult with his wife, delegate certain tasks and decisions to her, and defer to her instincts or preferences when he chooses. But the actual authority belongs to the husband. It is he who will give account to God for the oversight of the family.

The one limitation on the husband's authority is suggested by the principle of Colossians 3:18: "Wives, submit to your own husbands, as is fitting in the Lord." If at any point the husband's authority is not "fitting" (in the sense the apostle employs this word), the wife is not obliged to submit. Previously we noted that the apostle Paul repeatedly uses the Greek word translated "fitting" (*aneko*) to describe what is morally binding, and "not fitting" describes what God forbids. So if a husband tries to use his authority to command the wife to do something contrary to God's revealed Word, at that point he has overstepped the limits of his authority, and the wife is not even *permitted* to obey him. This same principle applies to *all* forms of authority: "We ought to obey God rather than men" (Acts 5:29).

You may recall, for example, an incident in the Book of Esther where Queen Vashti refused to dance a lewd dance before a drunken crowd (Esther 1:12). She was right to refuse.

What about a husband who is himself disobedient to the things of God and indifferent to Jesus Christ? Unless he commands the wife to disobey God, she should still obey him in all things.

What if he is unkind and unloving? What if he is neither good nor gentle? Should she still submit to him? As a matter of fact, she should. In fact, if she wants to win him to the Lord, her obedience is absolutely essential. The apostle Peter addresses this very issue in 1 Peter 3:1–5.

> Wives, likewise, be submissive to your own husbands, that even if some do not obey the word, they, without a word, may be won by the conduct of their wives, when they observe your chaste conduct accompanied by fear. Do not let your adornment be merely outward; arranging the hair, wearing gold, or putting on fine apparel; rather let it be the hidden person of the heart, with the incorruptible beauty of a gentle and quiet spirit, which is very precious in the sight of God. For in this manner, in former times, the holy women who trusted in God also adorned themselves, being submissive to their own husbands.

If your husband is disobedient to God or an unbeliever, even if he is utterly hostile to your faith and deliberately disobedient to the Word of God himself, God wants you to line up under that husband's authority (again, except in any matters where the husband commands you to disobey the Word of God).

Your obedience might be the very thing that wins him. Nagging him is not how God wants you to try to reach him for Christ. Browbeating him with Bible verses is not a wise tactic, either. The most effective testimony any wife can have in the eyes of an unbelieving husband is a meek and quiet submission to him (v. 1) set in a framework of "chaste conduct accompanied by fear" (v. 2).

The most attractive adornment for any wife is godly virtue placed against the backdrop of a meek and quiet spirit of submission. True beauty in a wife is never "merely outward; arranging the hair, wearing gold, or putting on fine apparel" (v. 3). What is truly attractive is that hidden person of the heart (v. 4), adorned with an incorruptible inward beauty and energized by a submissive spirit. By setting a godly example for an ungodly husband, the submissive wife *shows* him the power and beauty of the gospel through its effect in her own life. That is the most powerful means a woman has for winning a disobedient or unbelieving husband.

All this is doubly important when the wife is also a mother. By her testimony of godly submission, she can provide a good example for her children, giving them a Christ-honoring pattern in the midst of an environment where Christ is not always honored.

The ideal, of course, is for both parents to be mutually committed to the divine pattern for the family, working together in the proper order to raise their children in the nurture and admonition of the Lord.

The model father is someone like Joshua, not swayed by popular opinion or the flow of fashion, but willing to stand against everything carnal and compromising and boldly speak for his whole family: "If it seems evil to you to serve the LORD, choose for yourselves this day whom you will serve, whether the gods which your fathers served that were on the other side of the River, or the gods of the Amorites, in whose land you dwell. But as for me and my house, we will serve the LORD" (Joshua 24:15).

And the model mother is a woman like Hannah, whose deepest longings are apparently for her husband's and children's welfare, and who devotes her family to the LORD (1 Samuel 1) and devotes herself to caring for them.

Husband and wife, your marriage is the most important place

to live out your Christianity. If your Christianity is something reserved for Sunday worship only, your family will fail. But if you live your faith in the midst of your family, every day will be fruitful, productive, and blessed by God.

If you turn away from the principles of God's Word, your family life will be fraught with pain, disappointment, unfulfillment, sorrow, anger and every other fruit of disobedience. But if you follow the pattern God has set forth for the family, He promises His blessing.

Successful Parenting

Successful parenting cannot be achieved by following human techniques and child psychology. True success in parenting *only* results from faithful obedience to God's instructions for the family.

There is no better place, and certainly no more important place, for you to live out your faith than in your home. And if your home is not all it should be, it is undoubtedly because the principles of God's Word are not being followed there.

The family is the one environment where your devotion, faithfulness, and consistency matter most. It's where the most is at stake. It's where the greatest blessings can be realized. There is simply no greater earthly blessing than raising your children in a way that honors God, and then seeing them grow up to honor God with their own lives. May God grant that blessing in your family.

Appendices
Endnotes
Scripture Index
Subject Index

APPENDIX 1

❧

Jesus Wants Me for a Sunbeam?

BY PHIL JOHNSON[1]

*And these words, which I am commanding you today,
shall be on your heart. You shall teach them diligently to your
children, and shall talk of them when you sit in your house, when
you walk by the way, when you lie down, and when you rise up.*

—DEUTERONOMY 6:6–7

My earliest childhood memory is a pre-kindergarten Sunday school class. I suppose I was four years old—maybe even younger. Our church was an old, imposing building that smelled like someone's attic. The windows in our classroom were huge, and I loved the way the sun shone in. I was mesmerized by those little particles of dust that dance in the sunbeams in a dusty room.

I clearly remember one Sunday sitting in that room and learning the song "Jesus Wants Me for a Sunbeam." Our teacher eagerly pointed to the huge streams of light coming in the windows, and she tried to make them an object lesson.

The only trouble was, none of us understood anything about metaphors. All I could think of when we sang that song were those shiny little specks floating in the shaft of light, and I couldn't figure out *why* Jesus would want me to be one of those. I loved the song, but I have to admit it made no sense to me.

That memory is so deeply etched in my mind that even today

when I hear "Jesus Wants Me for a Sunbeam," I am immediately transported back to that old room with the big windows, and those little flecks of sunlit dust come to mind.

My own kids are now older than I was then, and one day several years ago it suddenly occurred to me that the earliest memories they would carry to adulthood had already been formed. Nearly everything they are learning now will stay with them for the rest of their lives. That's a scary thought for a parent.

Most Christian parents will admit to being somewhat intimidated by the weighty responsibility Scripture places on us. Our task is outlined in simple terms by verses like Proverbs 22:6: "Train up a child in the way he should go" and Ephesians 6:4: "Bring [your children] up in the training and admonition of the Lord."

Understanding our solemn duty as parents *ought* to provoke a certain amount of fear and trembling. Then again, it needn't paralyze us. Teaching spiritual truth to children is a joy. No one is more receptive, more hungry to learn, or more trusting than a child. Chances are, you'll never find more eager disciples than your own children. Don't squander the opportunity.

Let me suggest five practical principles to remember as you teach your children spiritual truth.

UNDERSTAND THAT CHILDREN CAN GRASP THE ESSENCE OF ALMOST ANY TRUTH

Among all the biblical admonitions for parents to teach their children the Word of God, not once is there a disclaimer or warning of any kind. There's no PG rating on Scripture—none of it is inappropriate for younger audiences. All Scripture is for all ages.

Don't hold back teaching your children because you think they aren't ready. Though they may not fully understand some of the more difficult spiritual concepts, children can grasp the essence of almost every truth. In fact, they are better equipped now to assimilate spiritual truth than they will be when they are older.

That's why Jesus called for childlike faith: "Assuredly, I say to you, whoever does not receive the kingdom of God as a child will by no means enter it" (Mark 10:15). What makes a child's faith different from an adult's? Simply that children refuse to be troubled by what they cannot understand.

Face it, few of us understand the concepts of infinity, eternity, or omnipotence any better than we did as children. We may speak of those ideas with more sophisticated terminology now, but our finite minds still cannot grasp the complete reality. Don't be afraid to admit that to your children.

When my youngest son, Jonathan, was in kindergarten, he was fascinated with the truth of God's omnipresence. He constantly tried to think of someplace God can't possibly be. "Dad, does God go to the Cubs' games?" he asked. I explained to him in simple terms what David said in Psalm 139:7–10, "Where can I go from Your Spirit? Or where can I flee from Your presence? If I ascend to heaven, You are there; If I make my bed in hell, behold, You are there. If I take the wings of the morning, if I dwell in the uttermost part of the sea, even there Your hand will lead me, and Your right hand shall hold me." I assured Jonathan that if God is in all those places, He must endure the Cubs' games, too.

And then I admitted to him that I'm just as baffled by this truth as he was. So was David. He wrote, "Such knowledge is too wonderful for me; it is high, I cannot attain it" (v. 6).

Amazingly, Jonathan was not the least bit troubled by my admission of ignorance. On the contrary, he seemed greatly comforted to know that he was not alone. He accepted the truth with the purest kind of faith.

AVOID FIGURATIVE LANGUAGE
AND UNEXPLAINED SYMBOLISM

Often adults, like the woman who taught me the sunbeam song, mistakenly believe an allegory or figure of speech will clarify some great truth. With children those things often only obscure the truth.

Unfortunately, the language most frequently used in children's evangelism suffers from this flaw. "Invite Jesus to come into your heart," we tell children. What child doesn't think of a red, valentine-shaped organ with a little door? It is actually easier and more precise to explain faith as complete trust and unconditional surrender. Most young children can grasp those ideas sooner than they can understand the metaphor of a door in their heart.

Children think in vivid imagery. When we talk, for example, of a heart dark with sin, the mental picture they see is quite literal. Ask a group of children to tell you what the song "Climb, Climb Up Sunshine Mountain" means. You'll begin to understand just how literally they think.

Nothing is wrong with using symbolism or figurative language to illustrate truth to children. Many excellent children's stories, fables, and fairy tales demonstrate how effective allegory can be. But all the symbolism must be carefully explained. Younger children especially do not have the ability to interpret figurative language independently.

CLEARLY SEPARATE REALITY FROM FANTASY

Children today are bombarded with fantasy and make-believe. Saturday morning television, super heroes, and fantasy toys have all reached unprecedented levels of popularity.

Even Sunday school curriculum feeds our kids huge doses of fantasy. Some of the finest material available includes stories of personified forest animals and other imaginary creatures.

There's nothing necessarily wrong with that approach. Fantasy can be a legitimate and valuable tool for teaching children. But don't neglect to draw the line clearly between what is reality and what is fantasy. If the lesson includes both a tale about Ronald Raccoon and the story of David and Goliath, make sure your kids know which story is make-believe and which one is actual history.

I'll never forget a conversation I had a few years ago with a three-year-old girl. "The Incredible Hulk" was her favorite television program. David Banner, the character who turns into the Hulk when he loses his temper, was the only David she knew anything about. She sat through an entire Sunday school lesson thinking he was the David her teacher was talking about. In the version of David and Goliath she recounted for me, David "hulked out" and ripped the giant's head off! It took me a while to sort the story out for her.

FIND OUT WHAT YOUR
CHILDREN ARE THINKING

Debrief your kids after Sunday school. It's great fun, and you'll find out exactly which truths they are learning and which ones are going over their heads.

One of the most interesting people I have ever known was a four-year-old named Holly. Her parents were our best friends, and my wife, Darlene, and I used to babysit her. Holly and I became close friends, and we had many profound conversations.

Holly was exceedingly well behaved and had an extraordinary interest in spiritual things. One day, however, she seemed determined to be naughty. I don't remember exactly what she was doing wrong. It was nothing serious, but it was out of character for her. After having to speak to her about her behavior several times, I asked in frustration, "Holly, what's wrong with you today?"

"I don't know," she sighed. "I just can't seem to get my life straightened out."

Her tone was so solemn and sincere that I had to suppress the urge to laugh. "Well, what's the problem?" I probed.

"I think it's the disciples' fault," she said in dead earnest.

Thinking she was talking nonsense to try to cover for herself, I spoke in a tone that said I was irritated: "Oh, come on, Holly. How could the disciples have anything to do with whether you misbehave or not?"

Her eyes got wide and she leaned forward as if to let me in on a deep secret. "They were *very* evil men."

Now I felt caught. I didn't want to dismiss the conversation without addressing this notion that the disciples were sinister, but I was reluctant to let her steer our talk away from the issue of her impish behavior. Knowing this had the potential to become a very long session, I nevertheless decided to deal with one issue at a time.

"The disciples were *not* evil men," I challenged her.

"Oh, yes," she corrected me. "They wouldn't let the little children come to Jesus."

"OK," I conceded, "they did wrong things sometimes, but they were mostly good men. They were Jesus' helpers."

"That's right," Holly said, as if she were the teacher and I were the student. "They *were* Jesus' helpers, but they tried to keep the children away. They were the bad guys." This was cut and dried to her, and she was visibly shocked at my willingness to defend anyone who would try to keep little children away from Jesus.

I quickly decided it would be prudent to abandon that part of the discussion. "Holly, the disciples were *not* evil," I said with finality. "But even if they were, I don't see what that has to do with your bad behavior."

She exhaled impatiently and explained, "I asked Jesus to come into my heart and wash away all my sin. I think He must have let the disciples help, and they didn't do a good job!"

Think about it. Holly's logic was impeccable. Using all the theological knowledge she had, she had concocted the most coherent explanation for sin in a Christian's life that her four-year-old mind could put together. In some ways it makes much more sense than the excuses we adults come up with. Yet I would never have understood what she was thinking if I hadn't kept asking questions.

DON'T EXPECT THEM TO GET
THE LESSON THE FIRST TIME

Holly and I had many discussions about the disciples after that, and it took me quite a long time to convince her that they weren't bad guys. But she came around.

Children rarely get the whole message right the first time. That's why the best Sunday school curriculum has a lot of built-in repetition and review.

My eldest son, Jeremiah, was only three when his Sunday school class began to have formal lessons. I loved having him retell the stories for me, and I was amazed at how accurate he was with most of the details. I was even more amazed that his little mind could absorb so much.

But he didn't always get the minutiae quite right.

One Sunday he was recounting Jesus' baptism for me. He rehearsed the narrative rapid-fire, without pausing to breathe: "Jesus came to this man, John, who baptized people, and He said, 'Baptize Me.' And John said he couldn't do it because he wasn't good enough, but Jesus said do it anyway."

"That's right," I said, congratulating myself that my son was such a good listener.

"So John baptized Jesus," Jeremiah continued. He lowered his voice to a dramatic whisper. "And then a very strange thing happened."

"What was it?" I whispered back.

"This big duck came down," he said.

I looked at the picture he had colored. Sure enough, John was baptizing Jesus while a bird descended from the sky. Jeremiah, who thought the teacher had said "duck" instead of "dove," had decorated his bird with mallard rings and an oversized beak.

Well, at least he had understood the core of the story. I was glad he had learned as much as he did. And he was quite impressed to discover that I already knew the story. He spent most of the afternoon pressing me for more details. By the time Jeremiah was six, he was something of an authority on John the Baptist. Now he's in his teens, teaching Bible lessons to other kids.

Deteronomy 6:6–7 records God's charge to the entire Jewish nation: "These words, which I am commanding you today, shall be on your heart. You shall teach them diligently to your children, and shall talk of them when you sit in your house, when you walk by the way, when you lie down, and when you rise up."

The principle still applies. Teaching our children spiritual truth is a never-ending, non-stop duty. But it is also a tremendous privilege and great joy. You are your child's primary spiritual guide. Don't back away from that role. Don't allow yourself to be intimidated or frustrated into abdicating this responsibility. It is the best thing about being a parent.

Appendix Two

Answering Some Key Questions about the Family

For several years I have been answering people's questions about parenting and family matters. Almost fifteen years prior to my writing this book, a collection of those questions was published in booklet form. This appendix is an updated version of that booklet. I include it here, even though many of the questions answered are covered much more in depth in the body of this book. The capsulized answers and the format of these "key questions" makes a nice summary and recap and a handy tool for parents seeking specific answers quickly.

APPENDIX 2

Answering Some Key Questions about the Family

Ours is a dark and decaying society. Sins that only twenty years ago were gasped at and spoken of in hushed and troubled tones are now publicly flaunted and even encouraged. Not so long ago, extramarital affairs were scandalous. Today, they're viewed as the norm. Even the president of the United States can engage in promiscuous behavior with a young intern, lie about it, and enjoy overwhelming support in public opinion polls. Why? Because so many Americans' own private lives are filled with similar sins. Our society has become inured to the sinfulness of sin. Homosexuality, incest, abortion, and even sex with children no longer shock and infuriate society the way they once did. In fact, all those sins now have their own advocacy groups, people who argue that such things are healthy, even desirable, activities.

The moral collapse has caused untold damage to the family. In fact, *any* attack on the moral fiber of society is ultimately an attack on the family. The proof can be seen in statistics that now show broken families are the rule rather than the exception. Turn on almost any one of the daytime television talk shows, and you're likely to see families literally disintegrating before your eyes.

Organized efforts to undermine the family and family life are now being sponsored by the women's rights movement, the children's rights movement, and the gay liberation movement. Hardly an election day comes anymore without including "gay marriage" initiatives and other voters' propositions whose sole purpose is to redefine the whole concept of family. These are perilous times for the family. Add into the sinister brew the changing concept of marriage, the increasing acceptance of divorce, and the obliteration of gender differences and elimination of any distinction between male-female roles, and it becomes easy to see why the concept of family today is nothing like it was just two decades ago.

The result is that families are disintegrating. Is there anyone left in our society who has not been touched in some way by divorce, child abuse, juvenile delinquency, and a host of other ills directly related to the breakdown of the family?

In every generation, the dissolution of marriages, torn families, and broken homes take a greater and greater toll. This generation's kids will reap what their parents have sown, and they'll plant seeds that will bear thirty, sixty, and a hundredfold. The rising numbers of ruptured families is now accelerating exponentially. What can we expect from future generations?

The only hope is for Christians to proclaim and reassert the divine standard from God's Word, and especially to live it out in their own family lives. Christians *must* hold firmly to the distinctive biblical pattern for the family. And the church must begin again to articulate without fear or shame what the Word of God says about the family.

In the early 1980s I made a film series and wrote a book about the family. The demand for that material exceeded everything I had ever written before that. And over the intervening years, wherever I have gone, people have asked me questions about the family. Despite the volumes that have been written and all that has been said about the family, Christians are still hungry for more instruction.

Recently, with the help of Word Publishing, I made an all-new videotape series on parenting to go with this book. Already the level of interest in that series has been astonishing, and people are clamoring for more. It's encouraging and exciting to see so many of God's people so keen to order their family lives according to His Word.

I must admit, however, that I don't particularly care to be cast as a "family expert." I don't believe any particular psychological or professional expertise is needed to help what ails modern families. The biblical principles governing the order of the family are amazingly simple and straightforward. Scripture sets forth the divine pattern for family life in such clear terms that whoever tries to follow the biblical pathway, though he be a fool, should not go astray (cf. Isaiah 35:8). The confusion comes when people try to fit the Bible's teaching into the framework of contemporary "wisdom." We must take God's Word at face value, and obey it without compromise or reservation.

This appendix cannot begin to answer *all* the biblical questions people will ask about the family, but these are some *key* questions. And my hope is that these answers will provide a starting point for dealing with the troubling questions you may be asking. The main portion of the book should fill in most of the details.

The family was God's first earthly institution. Before there was a government, and long before God instituted the church, He ordained marriage and the family as the basic building block of society. The destruction of the family we are witnessing today is, I believe, a harbinger of the ultimate collapse of our entire society. The more the family is threatened, the more society itself is in danger of extinction. We're living in the last days, and nothing shows that more graphically than the deterioration of the family.

Ephesians 5:22–6:4 contains a distillation of the biblical pattern for family life. There we read instructions for husbands, wives, children, and parents. In a few beautifully simple verses, God lays out everything we need to know and obey for a successful, harmonious family life:

> Wives, submit to your own husbands, as to the Lord. For the husband is head of the wife, as also Christ is head of the church; and He is the Savior of the body. Therefore, just as the church is subject to Christ, so let the wives be to their own husbands in everything.

> Husbands, love your wives, just as Christ also loved the church and gave Himself for her, that He might sanctify and cleanse her with the washing of water by the word, that He might present her to Himself a glorious church, not having spot or wrinkle or any such thing, but that she should be holy and without blemish. So husbands ought to love their own wives as their own bodies; he who loves his wife loves himself. For no one ever hated his own flesh, but nourishes and cherishes it, just as the Lord does the church. For we are members of His body, of His flesh and of His bones. "For this reason a man shall leave his father and mother and be joined to his wife, and the two shall become one flesh." This is a great mystery, but I speak concerning Christ and the church. Nevertheless let each one of you in particular so love his own wife as himself, and let the wife see that she respects her husband.

> Children, obey your parents in the Lord, for this is right. "Honor your father and mother," which is the first commandment with promise: "that it may be well with you and you may live long on the earth."

And you, fathers, do not provoke your children to wrath, but bring them up in the training and admonition of the Lord.

These, then, are the elements of a successful family: A wife characterized by submission; a husband who loves his wife sacrificially; children who obey and honor their parents; and parents who instruct and discipline their children by being a consistent, godly example. Virtually every question that can be asked about the family must first go back to this passage of Scripture and the pattern it sets forth.

Even if your family is without children, or without a father or mother, the basic formula for family success is the same: each family member must pursue his God-ordained role.

IF A WOMAN IS TO SUBMIT, ISN'T SHE PLAYING A LESSER ROLE?

Every member of the family, not just the wife, comes under the command to submit. In fact, it is significant to note that in the most reliable Greek manuscripts, no verb is used in verse 22 ("Wives, submit to your own husbands, as to the Lord"). The verb there is understood, and in order to make sense of the expression, the reader must refer back to verse 21 and borrow its verb (the Greek word for "submit," *hupotassō*). So a literal translation of verses 21–22 would be, " . . . submitting to one another in the fear of God. Wives, to your own husbands, as to the Lord."

Note that the command of verse 21 (submit to one another) actually applies to every member of the Body of Christ. Paul is saying there is a mutual submission in the Body of Christ that carries over into the family relationships. The husband shows his submission to the wife by his sacrificial love for her. His role is like that of Christ in John 13, where He girded Himself and washed the disciples' feet, accepting the lowest task it was possible for Him to perform on their behalf. The wife shows her submission to her husband by following his leadership, "For the husband is head of the wife, as also Christ is head of the church" (v. 23).

The husband's role is that of leader, "head of the wife." But that does not mean the wife is his slave, standing at his beck and call, awaiting commands like, "Do this! Get that! Go over here! Fix that for me!" and so on. The relationship between a husband and wife is one of "being heirs together of the grace of life" (1 Peter 3:7). The wife is the weaker vessel, and the husband is to honor her, protect her, and be an understanding leader.

The marital relationship is more intimate, personal, and inward than that of a master and slave. That is indicated in Ephesians 5:22 by the phrase "your own husbands." The husband-wife relationship is built on an intimate possessiveness. The verse seems to imply that it is assumed the wife would willingly respond in submission to one whom she possesses.

The wife's role is by no means second-class. It involves no kind of inferior status but only a God-ordained difference in function. This fact is wonderfully illustrated by 1 Corinthians 11:3: "The head of every man is Christ, the head of woman is man, and the head of Christ is God." God and Christ have roles of authority and submission, yet they are one in essence as God. So it is with husband and wife. Their roles differ, but in essential quality and value, they are equal. As Paul points out, men lead, but women are delivered from any thought of inferior influence by bearing and raising children. Men have the lead, but women have the stronger influence on the next generation (cf. 1 Timothy 2:11–15).

WHAT SHOULD A CHRISTIAN
WIFE DO IF HER HUSBAND FAILS TO BE THE
AUTHORITY FOR HER TO SUBMIT TO?

What if the husband isn't seeking to fulfill his role? What if he abdicates his position of leadership and leaves it to the wife to be the head of the home? It happens frequently, and especially in the realm of *spiritual* authority.

I once received a letter from a wife who wrote, "I've made a terrible mistake. I tried to be submissive to my husband, but he wouldn't take the leadership. Little by little I took it over, and now I'm dominating, and he will never take the leadership. How do I get myself out of this mess?"

The answer is, go back to being submissive. Force the issue. If he doesn't give you leadership to submit to, submit to the things you think he would like. Put yourself in the proper biblical role, and stay out of his. Then encourage him, pray for him, and support him as head of your home in every way you can. Above all, refuse to take dominant leadership of the family. Be obedient to the biblical pattern. Make suggestions and steer him quietly when absolutely necessary, but leave gaps for him to step into.

First Peter 3:1–2 says, "Wives, likewise, be submissive to your own husbands, that even if some do not obey the word, they, without a word, may be won by the conduct of their wives, when they observe your chaste conduct accompanied by fear." Again, the word translated "submissive" there is the Greek word *hupotassō*. It describes the function, not the essence, of the wife's role. In other words, while it is not saying that the wife's role is any less important than that of her husband, it is affirming that in the plan of God, she is the one to submit, and he is the one to take the headship.

Notice, too, that Peter says even if the husband is disobedient to the Word—whether he is a hostile Christ rejector or a believer who simply fails to take the leadership—the wife's response should still be submission.

So the best way a wife can encourage a non-leading husband to take his role as head of the family is simply to submit to him, pursue her role with greater determination and respect for him, and pray that the effect of that will be to push him closer to fulfilling his role.

HOW SHOULD A WIFE RESPOND TO A PHYSICALLY ABUSIVE HUSBAND?

Once I was taking questions from the audience in a meeting in Boston, and a young woman stood and asked how a Christian wife should deal with a husband who beats her. Immediately, a little eighty-nine-year-old, white-haired woman in the second row stood and shouted to her, "Hit him back, honey!"

Remembering the scene still makes me smile (I noticed after the meeting that the little old lady was wearing black boots). As funny as it was, however, I don't think she had the proper remedy.

Divorce is not always an option, either. Scripture does not automatically permit divorce in the case of a physically abusive husband.

Still, while Scripture does not specifically instruct the battered wife, it gives principles that certainly apply to her. Proverbs 14:16 says, "A wise man is cautious and turns away from evil" (NASB). God gives us wisdom to be defensive and cautious. We duck when something flies through the air at our heads. Common sense tells us to avoid situations where we're placed in physical danger. And I believe that is what God expects of us.

A woman whose husband brutalizes her is not only justified if she protects herself; she would be wrong not to. There is no virtue in a wife's willingly submitting to beatings and physical abuse from a cruel or drunken husband. And certainly there is no biblical warrant for a woman knowingly to allow herself to be beaten and even injured in the name of submission to her husband, especially if there are legitimate steps she can take to avoid it.

By way of comparison, the apostle Paul says in Romans 13 that we are to submit to civil government as a God-ordained authority. Yet that "submission" does not necessarily include voluntarily suffering at the hands of an abusive government. Our Lord said, "Whenever they persecute you in this city, flee to the next" (Matthew 10:23), certainly giving the persecuted warrant to flee the persecution of wicked governments if a way of escape is open. So the "submission" God calls us to does not include automatic acquiescence to sheer physical brutality.

My advice to women who are in danger of physical injury from their husbands is, first of all, to try to defuse the situation. Be careful not to provoke any circumstances that will make your husband become violent. Proverbs 15:1 says, "A soft answer turns away wrath."

This is certainly not to suggest women are to blame when their husbands become violent. There is no excuse whatsoever for a man to use physical violence against his wife; in fact, that is the most blatant kind of disobedience to the command given husbands in Ephesians 5:25. Men who physically abuse their wives cannot legitimately claim that *any* action on the wife's part justifies their use of brute force. To physically attack one's wife is an inexcusable and unconscionable sin against her and against Christ. And to try to defend such violence, as some men do, by claiming on biblical grounds that the husband is the "head" of the wife is to corrupt the very idea of headship. Remember that God is the head of Christ, and Christ is also the head of the church (1 Corinthians 11:3). So the expression involves not only leadership and authority, but also loving nurture and protection. "The husband is head of the wife, *as also Christ is head of the church;* and He is the Savior of the body" (Ephesians 5:23). The husband who thinks his headship justifies a domineering, tyrannical, or brutal leadership has no grasp of the biblical concept of headship.

If a violence-prone husband becomes agitated and abusive, the wife should remove herself from danger by leaving the home if necessary. God has promised that He will not test us beyond our ability to endure but will always make a way of escape (1 Corinthians 10:13). Sometimes escape is the *only* way. If you have children, and they are in danger, take them someplace where you will be secure until you feel you may safely come back.

If you are not truly in any physical danger but are merely a weary wife who is fed up with a cantankerous or disagreeable husband, even if he is an unbeliever who is hostile to the things of God, God's desire is that you stay and pray and sanctify that husband by your presence as a beloved child of God (1 Corinthians 7:10–16). The Lord will protect you and teach you in the midst of the difficult time.

Of course, pray for your husband, submit to him in every way you can, encourage him to seek advice and counsel from other biblically knowledgeable men, and do everything you can to heal the problems that cause him to be angry or abusive.

SHOULD A WIFE BE EMPLOYED OUTSIDE THE HOME?

The question of working wives is not one that can be answered with a simple yes or no. The real issue is how we understand the biblical priorities for a woman. Titus 2:4–5 says that the aged women in the church should teach the younger women "to love their husbands, to love their children, to be discreet, chaste, homemakers, good, obedient to their own husbands, that the word of God may not be blasphemed."

Clearly, the priority for any woman is caring for the needs of her family, and she does that first of all by being a "homemaker." First Timothy 5:14 emphasizes the same point, although a different Greek word is used. There, Paul writes, "I desire that the younger [women] marry, bear children, manage the house, give no opportunity to the adversary to speak reproachfully." The word translated "manage the house" in that verse is the Greek word *oikodespoteō*, which literally means "rule the home." The woman's domain is the home, and that is where a mother's priorities should always lie.

When the psalmist, under the inspiration of the Holy Spirit, wanted to show the glorious character of God, he could find no greater commendation than to say,

> Who is like unto the LORD our God,
> who dwelleth on high,
> Who humbleth himself to behold the things
> that are in heaven, and in the earth!
> He raiseth up the poor out of the dust,
> and lifteth the needy out of the dunghill;
> That he may set him with princes,
> even with the princes of his people.
> *He maketh the barren woman to keep house,*
> and to be a joyful mother of children.
> Praise ye the LORD
> (Psalm 113:5-9, KJV, emphasis added).

That is the ultimate thing God can do for a woman!

Caring for the home involves bearing children, training them, and managing the affairs of the home. All of that is a gift of God's grace to the woman. It is inextricably linked to the principle of the woman's being submissive to *her own husband*. If she works outside the home, she has a different set of circumstances with which to deal. She becomes accountable and submissive not only to her husband, but also to her boss at work. Other priorities often threaten the biblical priority of home and family, and a woman usually finds herself torn between fulfilling her biblical role and fulfilling a quite different role required by her job.

There is nothing in Scripture, however, that specifically forbids women from working, as long as they are fulfilling the priority in the home (Proverbs 31).

Whether a woman works outside the home or not, however, God's *primary* calling for her is to manage the home. It is the most exalted place for a wife. The world is what calls so many modern women out of the home, not the Lord. His Word portrays the woman's role as one preoccupied with domestic duties. It is a high calling, far more crucial to the future of a woman's children than anything she might do in an outside job.

The ultimate decision is a personal one that each woman must make in submission to her husband's authority. Obviously, a single woman would be free to work and pursue outside employment. A married woman with no children is perhaps a little more restricted in the amount of time and energy she can devote to an outside job. A woman who is a mother obviously has primary responsibility in the home and would therefore not be free to pursue outside employment to the detriment of the home. In fact, from my perspective as a parent, it is difficult to see how a mother could possibly do all that needs to be done in the home with the upbringing of children, hospitality, care of the needy, and work for the Lord (cf. 1 Timothy 5:3–14) and still work in an outside job.

WHAT ABOUT A WOMAN WHO WANTS TO WORK AT HOME, BUT WHOSE HUSBAND INSISTS THAT SHE WORK IN AN OUTSIDE JOB?

There are many women who face the dilemma of having husbands who demand that they work outside the home, although they themselves feel compelled by God to make the home the greater priority. In such a case, there is a tension between two biblical principles—submission (Ephesians 5:22) and God's plan for wives (1 Timothy 5:14; Titus 2:4–5).

The first approach for such a woman is to pray and then to share her conviction with her husband. In a loving way, she should let him know how deeply her obedience to God matters. It may be, if money is the issue, that she can find some creative way to earn money by work that can be done in the home, or by limiting her outside working time to hours when the kids are in school. (The godly woman mentioned in Proverbs 31 earned money through the work she did at home.) She may do a little study for her husband on the actual financial benefits of her working. Many studies reveal that a working wife often does not increase real spendable income at all, once child-care costs and other expenses are figured into the equation.

If the husband still insists that she work outside the home, she should obey him in a spirit of gentleness and keep praying. She should lovingly keep him aware of the negative impact on their relationship, the quality of the home, and the children's development. First Peter 3:1–6 gives added insight into a delicate situation like this. There, the wife is instructed to demonstrate her submission to God by submitting to the leadership of her husband, even if he is disobedient to the Word. Many women do manage to submit to their husbands and work outside the home, yet simultaneously obey God's Word by being a good keeper of the home between work hours. It's not easy, by any means, but a resourceful woman can manage to do it. By her submission to the husband, that wife is also submitting to the will of God. The Lord knows the circumstances, and He is able to work in the heart of the husband to change it.

WHAT ARE SOME PRACTICAL WAYS HUSBANDS CAN LOVE THEIR WIVES?

It's interesting that Ephesians 5:25 *commands* husbands to love their wives. First, it demonstrates that real love is not just a feeling that comes upon a person; it is an act of the human will. If it were not an act of the will, God would not command us to do it. Also, Paul doesn't say, *"Rule* your wives." There is a headship and one who follows, but the husband's perspective of his role should be focused not on the aspect of his authority, but on the aspect of sacrificial love for his wife.

Even more interesting than the command itself, though, is the standard of love that is set before husbands. The verse says, "Love your wives, just as Christ also loved the church and gave Himself for her." It is the most selfless, giving, caring kind of love conceivable to the human mind. There is no room in this kind of love for lording it over the wife or selfishly dominating the family.

Peter describes the husband's love for his wife: "Husbands, likewise, dwell with them with understanding, giving honor to the wife, as to the weaker vessel, and as being heirs together of the grace of life, that your prayers may not be hindered" (1 Peter 3:7). I see three key concepts in that verse.

The first is *consideration.* We are to live with our wives "in an understanding way." We must be sensitive, understanding, and considerate. The counseling staff in our ministry is familiar with all these complaints from unhappy wives: "He never understands me." "He doesn't know where I am." "He's insensitive to my needs." "We never talk." "He doesn't comprehend my hurts." "He speaks unkindly to me." "He doesn't treat me with love," and so on. Those women are saying that their husbands are inconsiderate, concerned more with what they get out of marriage than with what they give to it.

A second way of showing love to your wife is through *chivalry.* Remember, husband, your wife is a weaker vessel. A major part of your headship is your responsibility to protect her, care for her, and give yourself for her. This kind of caring, giving attitude can be expressed in many ways, often through seemingly insignificant gestures that nevertheless speak volumes to your wife about your love for her. You can open the car door for her, instead of backing down the driveway while she's still got one foot hanging out the door. Or simply bring her flowers. Small, frequent expressions of care mean more to a wife than a once-a-year special treatment on your anniversary.

Finally, husbands can show love to their wives by *communion* together. Notice, again, how Peter calls husbands and wives "heirs together of the grace of life." Marriage, more than any other kind of human institution, is designed to be a close partnership, a uniting of two into one. The fellowship of a married couple, then, needs to be as deeply intimate as it can be. And that is something that needs to be pursued with diligence; it requires a special effort. Husbands, commune with your wives. Talk to them. Share your spiritual lives together.

WHY MUST CHILDREN BE MADE TO OBEY?

Scripture is clear that children are to obey their parents. The Fifth Commandment says children are to honor their parents. At least a dozen verses in the Book of Proverbs alone tell children to obey their parents. Ephesians 6:1–3 says, "Children, obey your parents in the Lord, for this is right. 'Honor your father and mother,' which is the first commandment with promise: 'that it may be well with you and you may live long on the earth.'"

Why must children obey? Because they lack maturity in four major areas of life that are essential for independence. Those are delineated for us in Luke 2:52. There we are told how Jesus grew as a child in all four ways: "Jesus increased in wisdom and stature, and in favor with God and men." Even though He was perfect and sinless, our Lord grew as a child mentally, physically, socially, and spiritually. Those are the four ways *all* children need to grow.

Children need growth in *mental maturity*. Children lack wisdom. They lack discretion, instruction, and knowledge. When a baby is born into the world, his brain is almost completely without information. Whatever he's going to know must be taught to him. He doesn't know what is right and wrong; he doesn't know the right foods to eat; he doesn't know what not to put into his mouth; and he doesn't even have enough sense to stay out of the street. All those things must be taught, and childhood is a time for learning them.

Children also lack in the area of *physical maturity*. They are born weak and unable to support themselves. It is a long process as they gain strength and coordination. At first they must be fed, changed, and burped. They can't fend for themselves or make it in the world alone. It is their parents' responsibility to protect them.

Children lack *social maturity*. The most dominant thing you notice about a child when he comes into the world is that he is totally selfish. He wants what he wants immediately, and he thinks everything in reach belongs to him. It is difficult to teach a child how to share, what to say at appropriate times, and how to be humble. None of those things come naturally to any child.

Finally, children need *spiritual maturity.* A child doesn't naturally grow to love God. Scripture suggests that even little children do have *some* innate knowledge of God (Romans 1:19), but without proper instruction, they will drift away. Their own depravity will draw them away. It is the parents' responsibility to steer them the *right* direction. Proverbs 22:6 says, "Train up a child in the way he should go, and when he is old he will not depart from it." Obedience on the part of the child is the tool that brings him to maturity in all the proper ways.

SHOULD CHILDREN OBEY EVEN UNGODLY PARENTS?

Not all parents desire to raise their children in the way of truth. But when Paul writes, "Children, obey your parents *in the Lord,*" he is saying that obedience is in the sphere of serving, pleasing, honoring, and worshiping the Lord. He is not saying that the responsibility to obey extends only to those children whose *parents* are "in the Lord."

The command for children to obey their parents is absolute, except where the parents' commands are counter to the clear commands of God's Word. If a parent asks a child to violate a clear commandment of the Scriptures, the truth of Acts 5:29 comes into play: "We must obey God rather than men." In such circumstances, the child must refuse to obey the parent's wishes, but not in a defiant or insolent way. And he should accept the consequences of his disobedience patiently and without a display of defiance or anger.

HOW CAN PARENTS KNOW THE RIGHT WAY TO BRING UP THEIR CHILDREN?

Ephesians 6:4 says, "And you, fathers, do not provoke your children to wrath, but bring them up in the training and admonition of the Lord." The mistake too many parents make is that they think godly training will happen by itself in a Christian family. It won't. Parents are to lead by example, carefully and in a planned way. Their responsibilities include training, instructing, nurturing, and disciplining their children according to the way of the Lord, while at the same time not goading their children to anger.

Parents are the key to each child's spiritual growth. Every person is born with a bent to sin, and depravity will take over, unless its grip on a child is broken by regeneration. The child must be "born again, not of corruptible seed but incorruptible, through the word of God which lives and abides forever" (1 Peter 1:23). Scripture's instructions to parents suggest that the best environment in which to nurture the seed of God's Word for our children is in a loving environment of discipline.

In a study conducted several years ago, sociologists Sheldon and Eleanor Glueck of Harvard University identified several crucial factors in the development of juvenile delinquency. They created a test that can, with about 90 percent accuracy, predict future delinquency of children five to six years old. They listed four necessary factors in preventing juvenile delinquency. First, the father's discipline must be firm, fair, and consistent. Second, the mother must know where her children are and what they are doing at all times and be with them as much as possible. Third, the children need to see affection demonstrated between their parents and from their parents to them. And fourth, the family must spend time together as a unit.[1]

Similar studies suggest that right parent-child relationships normally occur in contexts where the parents genuinely love one another, where discipline is consistent, where the child senses that he or she is loved, where the parents set a positive moral and spiritual example, and where there is a father who leads the family.

The bottom line is this: The example you live out before your children is what most affects them. Many parents make the mistake of being overly concerned about how they are perceived in the church and in the community, while completely disregarding the way they live before their children. Nothing makes the truth more distasteful to a child than to have a hypocritical or spiritually shallow parent who affirms the truth publicly but denies it in the home.

Parents, ours is a solemn and awesome responsibility, but it's also a wonderful privilege. One of the most fulfilling experiences in all the world is to have children committed to following the Lord, no matter what the cost, because they have seen the same commitment in us.

WHAT MAKES A MARRIAGE STRONG?

Marriage for two Christians is first of all a commitment to Jesus Christ and then to each other. Satan loves to destroy marriages, and the best insulation against his attacks is a deep, profound, mutually shared relationship with Jesus Christ and a commitment to obedience of God's Word. In the presence of that kind of commitment, I don't believe a marriage can fail.

But to expand on that, here are two principles that strengthen a marriage. First, concentrate on being who you should be on the inside, not just on what you say, what you have, or even how you look externally. Peter gives this principle to wives in 1 Peter 3:3–4, but it surely applies to husbands as well: "Do not let your adornment be merely outward; arranging the hair, wearing gold, or putting on fine apparel; rather let it be the hidden person of the heart, with the incorruptible beauty of a gentle and quiet spirit, which is very precious in the sight of God."

Everything you own will decay. Even the way you look continues to deteriorate with age. But "the hidden person of the heart" matures, develops, and grows more beautiful as we become more and more like Christ. If that's where the focus of your marriage is, your love for one another will grow stronger, too.

A second principle is this: Concentrate on learning who your spouse is. I have counseled many people whose marriages were faltering simply because they had never taken time to get to know each other. It's important to realize that no person, and no marriage, is perfect. If you're clinging in frustration to an ideal of what you want your spouse to be like, you are hurting your marriage. Abandon your idea of the perfect mate, and begin learning to understand and love the one you have. Live with your partner "with understanding" (1 Peter 3:7).

It is significant that Paul commands husbands to love their wives (Ephesians 5:25) and wives to love their husbands (Titus 2:4). The point is that, no matter whom you are married to, you can learn to love your spouse. The prevailing wind of contemporary thinking seems to be that love is simply something that just happens—it comes and goes. And when it's gone, people get divorced. How foreign that is to the idea of Scripture, which does not recognize even the possibility of incompatibility between two marriage partners! God simply commands husbands and wives to love each other. The feelings of initial attraction—the high-intensity impulses—will diminish in all marriages. But when commitment is cultivated, the reward of lifelong, loving friendship and fulfillment is far more satisfying.

Remember, the essence of marriage is that two people become one flesh. And one is the indivisible number. In Matthew 19:5 Jesus quoted Genesis 2:24: "Therefore a man shall leave his father and mother and be joined to his wife, and they shall become one flesh." The Hebrew word translated "be joined" refers to an unbreakable bond. At the same time it is an active verb that carries the idea of pursuing hard after something. It indicates that marriage is meant to be two people diligently and utterly committed to pursuing one another in love, bonded in an insoluble union of mind, will, spirit, and emotion.

In verse six Jesus went on to say, "What therefore God has joined together, let no man separate." Every marriage, whether it is a Christian union or a pagan one, whether it was entered into according to the will of God or not, is a miraculous work of God, and if you tamper with that union, you are undermining the work of God.

Every family rests on that basic truth, and the success of the family as a whole rises or falls on the couple's commitment to each other and to the permanence of the union.

The family is so important in the plan of God! He wants to make our families all they can be, and the success of the family should be a priority for every Christian. We cannot allow the world to press us into its mold of divorce, division, delinquency, and all that goes with the failure of the family. If Christians don't have families that stay together, children who are raised in the nurture and admonition of the Lord, parents who love each other, and homes that are centered on Christ, we can never reach the world with the gospel. On the other hand, if we cultivate those things and pursue them wholeheartedly, the world will sit up and take notice of us and of our Christ.

ENDNOTES

INTRODUCTION

1. John MacArthur, *The Family* (Chicago: Moody Press, 1981).

CHAPTER 1: SHADE FOR OUR CHILDREN

1. Associated Press (March 30, 1997).

2. *Milwaukee Journal Sentinal* (July 7, 1998).

3. Barbara Boyer, "Grossberg, Peterson Sent to Jail," *Philadelphia Inquirer* (July 10, 1998), 1.

4. Cited in *Washingtonian* magazine, August 1986, and *Vogue,* September 1989.

5. Cited in the *Washington Post,* November 13, 1983.

6. *Inhumane Society* (Fox Publications, n.d.)

7. David Cooper, *The Death of the Family* (New York: Pantheon, 1971).

8. Kate Millet, *Sexual Politics* (New York: Doubleday, 1970).

9. Hillary Clinton, *It Takes a Village* (New York: Simon & Schuster, 1996).

10. *Pantagraphy* (September 20, 1970).

11. Gore Vidal, *Reflections Upon a Sinking Ship: A Collection of Essays* (Boston: Little, Brown, 1969), 246–48.

12. *Matthew Henry's Commentary on the Whole Bible,* 6 vols. (Old Tappan, NJ: Revell, n.d.), 3:917.

13. Judith Rich Harris, *The Nurture Assumption: Why Children Turn Out the Way They Do* (New York: Free Press, 1998).

14. *Ibid.*, 351.

CHAPTER 3: GOOD NEWS FOR YOUR KIDS

1. A similar version of this gospel outline is included in my book *Faith Works* (Dallas: Word, 1993), 200–206. Parents wishing to study a systematic approach to the biblical doctrine of salvation should be able to glean much help from that book.
2. See Appendix 1, "Jesus Wants Me for a Sunbeam?"
3. A. W. Tozer, *The Root of the Righteous* (Harrisburg, PA: Christian Publications, 1955), 61–63.

CHAPTER 5: THE FIRST COMMANDMENT WITH A PROMISE

1. *Matthew Henry's Commentary on the Whole Bible*, 6 vols. (Old Tappan, NJ: Revell), 6:716.
2. John MacArthur, *The Vanishing Conscience* (Dallas: Word, 1994).

CHAPTER 6: THE NURTURE AND ADMONITION OF THE LORD

1. *Papyri Oxyrhynchus*, 4.744.
2. Haim Ginott, *Between Parent and Child* (New York: Macmillan, 1965), 72.
3. Ted Tripp, *Shepherding a Child's Heart* (Wapwallopen, PA: Shepherd, 1995).
4. *Ibid.*, 39.
5. *Ibid.*, 20.
6. American Medical Association News Update, August 13, 1997.
7. Penelope Leach, "Spanking: A Shortcut to Nowhere," http://cnet.unbca/orgs/prevention_cruelty/spank.htm.
8. Lynn Rosellini, "When to Spank," (*U. S. News and World Report*, April 13, 1998). The article is online at http://www.usnews.com/usnews/issue/980413/13span.htm.
9. *Ibid.*
10. *Ibid.*
11. Review by Psychologist Robert E. Larzelere.
12. Quote by Kevin Ryan, director of the Center for the Advancement of Ethics and Character, *New York Times*.

13. Mike A. Males, *The Scapegoat Generation: America's War on Adolescents* (Monroe, ME: Common Courage, 1996), 116.
14. Rosellini, *ibid.*

CHAPTER 7: THE FATHER'S ROLE
1. *Homilies on Ephesians,* Homily 20 (Ephesians 5:25).

APPENDIX 1: JESUS WANTS ME FOR A SUNBEAM?
1. Phil is Executive Director of Grace to You and helps with the editorial process in most of my books.

APPENDIX 2: ANSWERING SOME KEY QUESTIONS ABOUT THE FAMILY
1. *Unraveling Juvenile Delinquency* (Cambridge, MA: Harvard, 1950), 257–71.

Subject Index